A Choice of Chaucer's Verse

A Choice of
CHAUCER'S
Verse

Selected
with an introduction by
NEVILL COGHILL

*(in the original
with an accompanying paraphrase
in modern verse)*

FABER AND FABER

3 Queen Square

London

*First published in 1972
by Faber and Faber Limited
3 Queen Square London WC1
Printed in Great Britain by
Latimer Trend & Co Ltd Plymouth
All rights reserved*

ISBN 0 571 09691 3 (Faber Paper Covered Editions)

CONDITIONS OF SALE
This book is sold subject to the condition that it shall not, by way of trade or otherwise, be lent, re-sold, hired out or otherwise circulated without the publisher's prior consent in any form of binding or cover other than that in which it is published and without a similar condition including this condition being imposed on the subsequent purchaser

© *Introduction and verse paraphrase, Nevill Coghill* 1972
© *This selection, Faber and Faber* 1972

For Helen Heath

Contents

INTRODUCTION	*page* 12
Proem	20
1. THE BOOK OF THE DUCHESS: lines 291–442 (with omissions)	22
2. THE FORMER AGE	30
3. TROILUS AND CRISEYDE, Book III: lines 1–49	34
4. TROILUS AND CRISEYDE, Book III: lines 50–168	38
5. THE KNIGHT'S TALE: lines 775–1746 (with omissions)	46
6. THE KNIGHT'S TALE: lines 1625–1856 (with omissions)	52
7. TROILUS AND CRISEYDE, Book III: lines 1184–1400	60
8. THE WIFE OF BATH'S TALE: lines 253–308 (with omissions)	70
9. THE FRANKLIN'S TALE: lines 511–896 (with omissions)	74
10. THE KNIGHT'S TALE: lines 1885–1954 (with omissions)	90
11. TROILUS AND CRISEYDE, Book V: lines 1807–1869	94
12. THE KNIGHT'S TALE: lines 2129–2186	98
13. THE PARDONER'S TALE: lines 333–640	102
14. THE FRIAR'S TALE: lines 77–346 (with omissions)	114
15. THE PROLOGUE TO THE SUMMONER'S TALE: lines 1–42	128
16. THE PARLIAMENT OF FOWLS: lines 99–105	132
17. TROILUS AND CRISEYDE, Book II: lines 918–931	132

[8]

Contents

INTRODUCTION	*page* 12
Proem	21

THE GOLDEN WORLD

1. DREAM HUNT AT DAWN	23
2. THE FORMER AGE	31
3. HYMN TO HEAVENLY LOVE	35
4. TROILUS DECLARES HIS LOVE	39
5. A DUEL FOR LOVE	47
6. A TOURNAMENT FOR LOVE	53
7. A CONSUMMATION OF LOVE	61
8. THE IDEA OF A GENTLEMAN	71
9. WHICH BEHAVED BEST?	75

THE WORLDS OF HEAVEN, HELL AND DEATH

10. THE DEATH OF ARCITE	91
11. THE DEATH OF TROILUS	95
12. FIRST CAUSE AND LAST EFFECT	99
13. IN QUEST OF DEATH	103
14. HOW DEVILS MAKE A LIVING	115
15. HOW A FRIAR VISITED HELL	129

THE WORLD OF DREAMS

16. ONE THEORY OF THE NATURE OF DREAMS	133
17. A LADY DREAMS OF HER LOVER	133

18. TROILUS AND CRISEYDE, Book V: lines 1233–1288	134
19. THE NUN'S PRIEST'S TALE: lines 62–356 (with omissions)	136
20. THE SHIPMAN'S TALE: lines 158–192	152
21. THE PROLOGUE TO THE CANTERBURY TALES, THE PRIORESS: lines 118–162	154
22. THE PROLOGUE TO THE CANTERBURY TALES, THE WIFE OF BATH: lines 445–476	156
23. THE PROLOGUE TO THE CANTERBURY TALES, THE PARDONER: lines 675–706	158
24. THE PROLOGUE TO THE CANTERBURY TALES, THE PARSON: lines 477–528 (with omissions)	162
25. THE PROLOGUE TO THE CANTERBURY TALES, THE SQUIRE: lines 79–100	164
26. THE COOK'S TALE, THE APPRENTICE: lines 1–58	166
27. THE PROLOGUE TO THE CANTERBURY TALES, THE MILLER: lines 545–566	168
28. THE MILLER'S TALE: lines 3187–3854	170
29. THE CANON'S YEOMAN'S TALE: lines 750–937 (with omissions)	206
30. THE MERCHANT'S TALE: lines 93–110	212
31. THE MERCHANT'S TALE: lines 67–74	212
32. THE MERCHANT'S TALE: lines 278–310	214
33. THE MERCHANT'S TALE: lines 393–408	216
34. THE MERCHANT'S TALE: lines 411–438	218
35. THE WIFE OF BATH'S PROLOGUE: lines 1–614 (with omissions)	220
36. THE CLERK OF OXFORD'S TALE, LENVOY DE CHAUCER: lines 1177–1212	228
37. THE FRANKLIN'S TALE: lines 33–50	230
38. THE EPILOGUE (Balade de bon conseyl)	232
Envoy	234

18. A LOVER DREAMS OF HIS LADY	135
19. ARE DREAMS DIAGNOSTIC OR PROPHETIC?	137

THE WORLD OF PORTRAITURE

20. SELF-REVELATION OF A BONNE BOURGEOISE	153
21. MADAME EGLANTINE	155
22. THE WIFE OF BATH	157
23. A FUND-RAISER FOR THE CHURCH	159
24. A COUNTRY PARSON	163
25. AN ACCOMPLISHED YOUNG MAN	165
26. ANOTHER	167
27. A MILLER	169

THE STUDENT WORLD

28. THE MILLER'S TALE	171

THE WORLD OF SCIENCE

29. HOW TO BE AN ALCHEMIST	207

THE WORLD OF MATRIMONY

30. WHAT A BENEDICTION!	213
31. THE GIFT OF GOD	213
32. A MORE CAUTIOUS VIEW	215
33. TWO PERFECT KINDS OF BLISS	217
34. GOD'S WHIP	219
35. FROM THE MEMOIRS OF THE WIFE OF BATH	221
36. ANTHEM FOR MILITANT WIVES	229
37. WHEN LOVE BEATS HIS WINGS	231

EPILOGUE

38. FORTH, PILGRIM!	233
Envoi	235

Introduction

I

I have tried in this selection to give a taste of the finest things in Chaucer's poetry; they are taken, for the most part, from his great narrative poems, *Troilus and Criseyde* and *The Canterbury Tales*; he excelled in narrative. It is, however, a kind of excellence that is difficult to illustrate by short excerpts; I have therefore included *The Miller's Tale* in its entirety and the narratives that conclude *The Pardoner's Tale* and *The Summoner's Tale*, which are three of his briefer masterpieces in short-story writing, an art in which Chaucer has had no equal in English until Rudyard Kipling.

As well as being a great narrator, he was a great portrait-painter; indeed, he invented the word-portrait and the autobiographical monologue; some of his fine things in these *genres* I have tried to illustrate from *The Prologue to the Canterbury Tales* and from the Wife of Bath's tremendous preamble about her first five husbands.

I have, however, mainly guided my selection by the hope of showing the worlds he has opened to us, the range of his poetic vision, the scope of his interests; but there are many fine things I have been forced to leave out for lack of space, and I expect to incur the reproaches of many lovers of Chaucer for omitting altogether the things they would first have hoped to see; for there is room in Chaucer for many different first preferences. Yet, for those who know Chaucer less well (and it is to them that this book is mainly addressed) I hope this selection may pass muster and lead them enjoyably into the Chaucerian universe or, at least, into the taste of it.

It is not known when Geoffrey Chaucer was born; in an official deposition made by him in 1386 he declared himself to be *'del age de xl ans & plus'*, but how much was meant by that *'plus'* has been disputed. We shall be safe, however, to bracket his birth-year between 1340 and 1345. He was the son of a London wine-merchant; at an early age he became a page in a royal household, was briefly on Active Service in France (in the Hundred Years' War) and was taken prisoner in 1359; King Edward III helped to ransom him in 1360 and then employed him as a kind of courier on various missions abroad, including two to Italy (in 1372 and 1378), on which he was something more than a mere courier, rather, an assistant negotiator on state business concerning trade facilities. After his return from the second of these, he was promoted to become an important Customs Officer in London, Comptroller of the Customs and Subsidy of wools, skins and tanned hides (wool was then our principal export), and in time he became a Justice of the Peace and Knight of the Shire for Kent (1385/6). He married a lady-in-waiting to Queen Philippa in, or shortly before, 1366; her maiden name was Philippa de Roet and they had children, one of whom, called Thomas, grew up to be a large landowner and Speaker to the House of Commons (as it then was in its early, less-evolved form).

Some have doubted whether this Thomas Chaucer was the poet's son, but I think the evidence is good enough; he was indisputably the son of Philippa, for the de Roet arms on his splendid tomb at Ewelme, in Oxfordshire, proclaim it, and I repudiate the suspicion entertained by some scholars that Philippa was unfaithful to Geoffrey, and, like her sister Catherine, one of John of Gaunt's mistresses.

Geoffrey Chaucer's career as a courtier had advanced under the wing of King Edward III, and, later, under that of John of Gaunt, Edward's fourth son. Gaunt (Shakespeare's 'Old John of Gaunt') was uncle to King Richard II (who succeeded to King Edward, his grandfather), and it was at the Court of Richard II that Chaucer spent most of his working-life as a royal official, and where he used also to read his poems aloud (though he does not appear to have been paid for doing this) either in the garden on long summer evenings, or perhaps in the great hall, round the fire in the winter.

Richard was deposed and murdered in 1399, and was succeeded by Henry IV, son of Gaunt and of his first wife, Blanche, Duchess of Lancaster. Chaucer's first original poem on a large scale, *The Book of the Duchess*, was an elegy on her death, which occurred in 1369; a wonderful piece, as will be seen from the extract which opens this book. What is likely to have been Chaucer's last poem—a *Complaint to his Empty Purse*—was addressed to her son, Henry, on his accession to the throne in 1399.

The tenuous, but continuous family connection between Chaucer, the Plantagenets and the Lancastrians, was thus maintained; and still further maintained, it may be presumed, by a fact I have already mentioned. Catherine Swynford (*née* Catharine de Roet, sister of Philippa, the poet's wife) had for many years been John of Gaunt's mistress, and the governess of his children; in 1396 she became Gaunt's third wife and her children by him were legitimated by Parliament; by then, however, Philippa Chaucer had been dead many years, nine at least. The impoverished poet, during the last four years of his life, was thus a sort of uncle-by-marriage to the King he was addressing, since his dead wife had been sister to the King's beat-the-pistol step-mother; a tricky relationship in a disturbed Age.

To return from these family involvements to Chaucer's actual career as a courtier, he had attained a certain elevation (thanks largely to Gaunt's influence) by 1386; but in that year his patron left England to try for a crown in Spain, and was three years abroad; at home, Thomas Duke of Gloucester, youngest son of Edward III, took over the government, for the King (Richard II) was still in his minority, being under twenty-one. The Duke of Gloucester had no connection with Chaucer and so he displaced him from his position, and the poet lost all his jobs at Court in one fell swoop; in the following year (1387) Philippa died. It would seem as if these must have been his saddest, most anxious years; yet in them he began in earnest on *The Canterbury Tales* and continued with a huge poetic energy, which in the end seems to have flagged, to work on them, perhaps until the end of his life; he never managed to finish or finalize them in their proper order. In another poem written, it would seem, towards the end of his life (*L'Envoy de Chaucer a Scogan*) he tells us:

> Ne thinke I never of slepe wak my muse,
> That rusteth in my shethe stille in pees.
> Whyl I was yong, I putte hir forth in prees,
> But al shal passe that men prose or ryme;
> Tak every man his turn as for his tyme.

On Gaunt's return from Spain, Chaucer was restored to some degree of favour for a while, and was made Clerk of the King's Works; but after 1391 he dwindled back into a pensioner in straitened circumstances, under occasional pressure from creditors. He never regained his earlier affluence—if affluence it may be called—and he died and was buried in Westminster Abbey (perhaps because he then had a house in Westminster, perhaps because of his standing as a courtier, but not because of his poetry) on 24th October 1400.

II

A courtier by upbringing, a poet by genius, his poetry reflects the course of his professional life in certain large ways; both begin in the golden world of an aristocratic idealism famous for the refinements of the codes of love and war and courtesy that evolved within it, and for the Christian piety that it professed, in common with the rest of Christendom, whence it was derived. It was Chaucer's good fortune, too, to have been born in London during the years in which the English language, especially in its London form, was to emerge and claim supremacy over Norman French for all ordinary purposes. Speaking of his own 'light Englissh', Chaucer speaks also of King Richard II '*that is lord of this langage*'; the King's English had become the King's, fresh and new, and ready for Chaucer.

Apprenticed to the aristocratic, chivalric and romantic world that burst into flower in England during his boyhood, Chaucer's first vision of it is noble, natural and innocent, and finds expression (though with a deepening consciousness of its sorrows) in *The Book of the Duchess*, *The Knight's Tale* and *Troilus and Criseyde*; and it is from these poems, in the main, that I have sought to illustrate his Plantagenet qualities; but discoveries even greater than that of the Golden World lay before Chaucer. His daily work was at the heart of London commerce and of the whole busy, bourgeois world from which he had originally sprung. Taught by the life about him, his vision, which had deepened in *Troilus and Criseyde*, now gradually broadened; and, as it broadened it also became more detailed, sharper, more realist. He began to notice—but always with apparent good humour—the many self-contradictions between a man's profession and his behaviour; he became aware—one might almost say delightedly, ironically aware—of a certain blackguardism in humanity. Certainly there were some blackguards about ready to hand for his comment and description; but it would seem from what he tells us of them—the Pardoners, the Summoners, the Friars, the men of riot, and other such—that for all his awareness of their wickedness he had no real fear they would corrupt the world. They would meet their reward in due course, and he had a fair, comic idea of the kind of Hell in which some of them would meet it, as will be found in this book.

This, I think, underlies the cheerfulness of Chaucer's poetical vision of the world; he does not deny the evil in it, on the contrary he singles it out, often enough, and with acuity and relish; but the general good health of society and the general agreement as to the purpose of life, seen with lightest allegory as a *pilgrimage*, seems to have led him to think the evils he saw about him could be contained, as the pilgrimage moved along, without too much trouble; he did not share the view of his great contemporary, the author of *Piers Plowman*, that the Day of Anti-Christ was upon them. At least there is no hint of it in Chaucer, unless it be in the last lines of his poem *The Former Age*. Mainly, however, Chaucer was able to keep cheerful, to feel secure, to mingle happily with all kinds and classes of men and women, with trenchant yet amused understanding, and no lack of charitable sympathy in his wit, and sense of fun.

As well as a vision of the noble, the peasant and the bourgeois worlds and codes, all three of which meet and mingle in *The Canterbury Tales* in quarrelsome amity, we see, or catch glimpses of, the surrounding universe, in Ptolemaic terms and teeming references to the planetary gods; and there are glimpses also of Heaven and Hell, the former serious, the latter comic; this is in the general medieval tradition, to be seen in so many church carvings and manuscript illuminations; *devils are comics*—horror-comics, perhaps, yet still comics; but sanctity is serious.

There is also the surrounding world of Nature, most famously pictured in the lines that open *The Canterbury Tales*, but here chiefly seen in a passage from *The Book of the Duchess* which seems to me the freshest start a poet ever made into the dewy light of dawn, in a noble world, at the spring of the year. I can scarcely think of any other work of poetry unless it be in *Love's Labour's Lost*, where there is such an impulsive freshness of feeling, such a sense of wonder and joy in the excitement of being alive and young in pleasant company, and a world full of beauty and adventure, sport and fine feeling, kindness and conversation.

Since I have offered shortage of space as an excuse for not including certain poems in their entirety, it will be asked why I have halved the possible contents of the book by offering a modern verse-paraphrase opposite every page of the original text. The answer is that this selection is designed to draw readers who believe they cannot read Chaucer's poetry as he wrote it into the circle of those who believe they can. Chaucer is neither so easy, nor so difficult to read as some have said: a point here and there demonstrated in this book. I have been told many times, and by many different people, that the archaic spelling, the uncertainties of metre, and the occasional difficulties of idiom and vocabulary in the original call for an extra effort of attention, a kind of reading-vigilance that demands footnote and glossary work, and which robs the reader of a cursive pleasure he feels entitled to, especially in great narrative art; Chaucer for them becomes too much like hard work, they say, whereas he should be wonderfully easy and pleasant.

One way of learning to skate with ease is to lean on a chair pushed over the ice before one; clumsy as the chair is, it gives support to self-confidence and stills trepidation in the future skater. The verse-paraphrases here supplied are offered as chairs for future Chaucerians; they are as good as I have known how to make them; those who do not need them can skate happily away into Chaucer without them; others can use them until confidence in their ability to read the original has been established and they feel themselves able to follow at equal speed and with greater pleasure, sounding his magical language in their minds. The text of Chaucer's original here printed is that of Walter Skeat (1894-7) which I have mainly used in making the paraphrases.

As a giver of pleasure to his readers I know of no equal to Chaucer, unless it be Dickens at his best; in the brilliance of their narrative and the richness in presenting human nature, and in the Christian cheerfulness they share (in spite of a thousand theological differences, no doubt) they have much in common; and the sense of *pleasure*, the delight in life, crowns all. There are, of course, large areas they do not share. There is more evil in the world of Dickens, and it can have tragic dimensions; Chaucer's tragic sense did not reach beyond pathos. On the other hand, compared with Chaucer, Dickens knew nothing about women. For Chaucer they formed a large part of his comic vision of human relationships.

It may be for his lack of tragic sense in Chaucer that some readers, even fine ones like Matthew Arnold, have thought he lacked 'High Seriousness'; for many think that comedy cannot paint so true a picture of the world as tragedy. But there are others, even among the gravest of men, who have thought, like Dante, that a happy ending to all things was in our power by the grace of God, and that therefore a tale with a happy ending was just as philosophical an image of life, as serious, and in the long term truer, than one ending in sorrow and despair. But it takes courage as well as other virtues (such as faith, hope and charity) to think like this, with all the evidence of human grief and wickedness that stares us in the face. They stared Chaucer in the face too; he was born into the Age of the Black Death, the Hundred Years' War, the Great Schism, sporadic famine, the Peasants' Revolt, its brutal suppression, and a multitude of political murders culminating with that of Richard II, for whom he had worked so long; yet he maintained and communicated a cheerfulness and warmth of heart so powerfully that we can feel them still, and even take them into our own lives, difficult as they are.

ACKNOWLEDGEMENT

The translation of *The Former Age* (p. 31) is reprinted from *Essays and Poems Presented to Lord David Cecil*, edited by W. W. Robson, 1970.

Proem

*Whan that Aprill with his shoures sote
The droghte of Marche hath perced to the rote,
And bathed every veyne in swich licour,
Of which vertu engendred is the flour;
Whan Zephirus eek with his swete breeth
Inspired hath in every holt and heeth
The tendre croppes, and the yonge sonne
Hath in the Ram his halfe cours y-ronne,
And smale fowles maken melodye,
That slepen al the night with open ye,
(So priketh hem nature in hir corages):
Than longen folk to goon on pilgrimages
And palmers for to seken straunge strondes
To ferne halwes couth in sondry londes;
And specially, from every shires ende
Of Engelond, to Caunterbury they wende,
The holy blissful martir for to seke,
That hem hath holpen whan that they were seke . . .*

Proem

*When in April the sweet showers fall
And pierce the drought of March to the root, and all
The veins are bathed in liquor of such power
As brings about the engendering of the flower,
When also Zephyrus with his sweet breath
Exhales an air in every holt and heath,
Upon the tender shoots, and the young sun
His half-course in the sign of the Ram has run,
And the small fowl are making melody
That sleep away the night with open eye
(So nature pricks them and their heart engages)
Then people long to go on pilgrimages,
And pilgrims long to seek the stranger strands
Of far-off saints, hallowed in sundry lands,
And specially from every shire's end
Of England, down to Canterbury they wend,
To seek the holy, blissful martyr, quick
To give his help to them when they were sick.*

1. *The Book of the Duchess*

lines 291–442, with omissions

ME thoughte thus:—that hit was May,
And in the dawninge ther I lay,
Me mette thus, in my bed al naked:—
I loked forth, for I was waked
With smale foules a gret hepe,
That had affrayed me out of slepe
Through noyse and swetnesse of hir song
And, as me mette, they sate among,
Upon my chambre-roof withoute,
Upon the tyles, al a-boute,
And songen, everich in his wyse,
The moste solempne servyse
By note, that ever man, I trowe,
Had herd; for som of hem song lowe,
Som hye, and al of oon acorde.
To telle shortly, at oo worde,
Was never y-herd so swete a steven,
But hit had be a thing of heven;—
So mery a soun, so swete entunes,
That certes, for the toune of Tewnes,
I nolde but I had herd hem singe;
For al my chambre gan to ringe
Through singing of hir armonye.
For instrument nor melodye
Was nowher herd yet half so swete,
Nor of acorde half so mete;
For ther was noon of hem that feyned
To singe, for ech of hem him peyned
To finde out mery crafty notes;

[22]

THE GOLDEN WORLD

1. *Dream Hunt at Dawn*

It seemed to me that it was May,
And in the dawning as I lay
All naked in my bed, I dreamed
I had been woken (so it seemed)
By little birds; there was a heap
Of them that had disturbed my sleep
By the noise and sweetness of their song;
And (so I dreamed) they made a throng
Upon my chamber-roof without,
Upon the tiles and all about,
And each according to his throat,
Sang a festal service, note
By note, the sweetest (so thought I)
Man ever heard; and some sang high
And some sang low, in sweet accord;
To tell you shortly, never poured
So sweet a voice, so freely given,
Unless it were a thing from Heaven,
So merry a sound, so sweet a newness
Of noise, that, for the town of Tunis,
I would not have forgone their singing;
For all my chamber was set ringing
By what they sang in harmony.
No instrument of melody
Ever sounded half so sweet,
Or in a concord so complete;
Not one among them all was feigning
To sing, but, rather, each was straining
To find out merry, crafty notes;

They ne spared not hir throtes.
And, sooth to seyn, my chambre was
Ful wel depeynted, and with glas
Were al the windowes wel y-glased,
Ful clere, and nat an hole y-crased,
That to beholde hit was gret joye.
For hoolly al the storie of Troye
Was in the glasing y-wroght thus,
Of Ector and king Priamus,
Of Achilles and Lamedon,
Of Medea and of Jason,
Of Paris, Eleyne, and Lavyne.
And alle the walles with colours fyne
Were peynted, bothe text and glose,
Of al the Romaunce of the Rose.
My windowes weren shet echon,
And through the glas the sunne shon
Upon my bed with brighte bemes,
With many glade gilden stremes;
And eek the welken was so fair,
Blew, bright, clere was the air,
And ful atempre, for sothe, hit was;
For nother cold nor hoot hit nas,
Ne in al the welken was a cloude.

And as I lay thus, wonder loude
Me thoughte I herde an hunte blowe
T'assaye his horn, and for to knowe
Whether hit were clere or hors of soune.

I herde goinge, up and doune,
Men, hors, houndes, and other thing;
And al men speken of hunting,
How they wolde slee the hert with strengthe,
And how the hert had, upon lengthe,
So moche embosed, I not now what.
Anon-right, whan I herde that,
How that they wolde on hunting goon,

They did not spare their little throats.
My chamber (it had come to pass)
Was brightly painted; there was glass
In all the windows, clear and fair,
—Not a hole broken anywhere—
So looking at it was a joy,
For the entire Tale of Troy
Was pictured in the glazing thus:
Sir Hector and King Priamus,
Achilles and Laomedon,
Medea and Jason; further on
There was Lavinia to be seen
And Helen, Menelaus' Queen,
With Paris; there were paintings too
On all the walls—their colours new—
With text and commentary prose
Of the whole *Romance of the Rose*.

  Shut were my windows, every one,
And through the glass there shone the sun
Upon my bed with brightening beams,
In many glad and golden streams;
And then the sky itself was fair,
Blue and bright and clear the air,
And it was truly temperate,
Nor hot, nor cold, but delicate;
In all the sky there was no cloud.

  As thus I lay, a horn blew loud;
It seemed as if the huntsman blew
To try his horn, if it were true
And clear, or whether hoarse in sound;
And I heard goings up and round
Of hound and horse, with men in front,
And all were talking of a hunt
—How they would slay the hart in strength,
And how the hart had run, at length,
To cover, and I don't know what;
But when I heard it, up I got,
For they were saying they would go

I was right glad, and up anoon;
[I] took my hors, and forth I wente
Out of my chambre; I never stente
Til I com to the feld withoute.
Ther overtook I a gret route
Of huntes and eek of foresteres,
With many relayes and lymeres,
And hyed hem to the forest faste,
And I with hem;—so at the laste
I asked oon, ladde a lymere:—
'Say, felow, who shal hunte[n] here?'
Quod I; and he answerde ageyn,
'Sir, th'emperour Octovien,'
Quod he, 'and is heer faste by.'
'A goddes halfe, in good tyme,' quod I,
'Go we faste!' and gan to ryde.
Whan we came to the forest-syde,
Every man dide, right anoon,
As to hunting fil to doon.
The mayster-hunte anoon, fot-hoot,
With a gret horne blew three moot
At the uncoupling of his houndes.
Within a whyl the hert [y]-founde is,
Y-halowed, and rechased faste
Longe tyme; and at the laste,
This hert rused and stal away
Fro alle the houndes a prevy way.
The houndes had overshote hem alle,
And were on a defaute y-falle;
Therwith the hunte wonder faste
Blew a forloyn at the laste.

I was go walked fro my tree,
And as I wente, ther cam by me
A whelp, that fauned me as I stood,
That hadde y-folowed, and coude no good.
Hit com and creep to me as lowe,
Right as hit hadde me y-knowe,
Hild doun his heed and joyned his eres,

[26]

A-hunting, and this pleased me so
I took my horse, and forth I went
Out of my chamber, with intent
To join them in the field without;
And soon I overtook a rout
Of foresters and huntsmen there,
With hounds on leash and hounds to spare,
All hurrying—and I with them—fast
Towards the forest; so, at last,
To one who led a hound in front
I spoke and said 'Whose is this hunt,
Good fellow?' 'Sir', replied the man,
'The Emperor Octovian
Is not far off, and it is his.'
'By God, and lucky that it is!
Let's hurry!' I began to ride
And when we reached the forest side
Each one of them at once began
His business as a hunting man.
The Master Huntsman, working fast,
Blew his horn with triple blast;
Uncoupled then was every hound.

Within a while the hart was found,
Hallooed and headed back again
For quite a time, but all in vain;
The hart was roused and, stealing back,
Escaped them by a secret track
And so the hounds were brought to halt,
They'd overshot and were at fault.
The Huntsman then, with no delay,
Blew a hasty 'Gone Away!'

I had walked onward from my tree,
When up there came a whelp to me
And fawned upon me where I stood,
Had followed, but could do no good.
It came and humbly crept to own me
Just as if the whelp had known me,
Joined his ears, laid down his head,

And leyde al smothe doun his heres.
I wolde han caught hit, and anoon
Hit fledde, and was fro me goon;
And I him folwed, and hit forth wente
Doun by a floury grene wente
Ful thikke of gras, ful softe and swete,
With floures fele, faire under fete,
And litel used, hit seemed thus;
For bothe Flora and Zephirus,
They two that make floures growe,
Had mad hir dwelling ther, I trowe;
For hit was, on to beholde,
As thogh the erthe envye wolde
To be gayer than the heven,
To have mo floures, swiche seven
As in the welken sterres be.
Hit had forgete the povertee
That winter, through his colde morwes,
Had mad hit suffre[n], and his sorwes;
Al was forgeten, and that was sene.
For al the wode was waxen grene,
Swetnesse of dewe had mad it waxe.

  Hit is no need eek for to axe
Wher ther were many grene greves,
Or thikke of trees, so ful of leves;
And every tree stood by him-selve
Fro other wel ten foot or twelve.
So grete trees, so huge of strengthe,
Of fourty or fifty fadme lengthe,
Clene withoute bough or stikke,
With croppes brode, and eek as thikke—
They were nat an inche a-sonder—
That hit was shadwe over-al under;
And many an hert and many an hinde
Was both before me and bihinde.
Of founes, soures, bukkes, doës
Was ful the wode, qnd many roës,
And many squirelles, that sete

[28]

And smoothed his hackles; I was led
To try and catch it, whereupon
It fled away, and it was gone.
I followed it; the journey lay
Down by a green and flowery way,
Thick in grasses soft and sweet,
Many fair flowers at my feet,
And little used (or so I dreamed);
For Zephyrus and Flora seemed
To have made their dwelling there—you know,
Those two that make the flowers grow.
It was indeed, to look at it,
As if the world had had the wit
To show itself as gay as heaven,
And have more flowers than the seven
Such stars that deck the firmament;
Forgotten were the frosts of Lent,
The poverty of wintry morrows
That made it suffer, and its sorrows;
All was forgotten, I could see;
For green again was every tree,
Sweetness of dew had made it grow.

You need not ask, for well you know,
If there were many groves of green
Thick with trees and leafy sheen;
And by itself stood every tree,
Ten foot apart, or twelve maybe,
From every other, huge of strength,
Forty or fifty fathom in length,
Clean without a bough or stick,
With tops as broad as they were thick
—They were not an inch asunder—
So there was shade on all thereunder;
Many a hart and many a hind
There were, before me and behind,
Fawns and sorels, bucks and does,
Filled the wood, and many roes;
Many a squirrel had found seating

Ful hye upon the trees, and ete,
And in hir maner made festes.
Shortly, hit was so ful of bestes,
That thogh Argus, the noble countour,
Sete to rekene in his countour,
And rekene[d] with his figures ten—
For by tho figures mowe al ken,
If they be crafty, rekene and noumbre,
And telle of every thing the noumbre—
Yet shulde he fayle to rekene even
The wondres, me mette in my sweven.

2. *The Former Age*

A blisful lyf, a paisible and a swete
Ledden the peples in the former age;
They helde hem payed of fruits, that they ete,
Which that the feldes yave hem by usage;
They ne were nat forpampred with outrage;
Unknowen was the quern and eek the melle;
They eten mast, hawes, and swich pounage,
And dronken water of the colde welle.

Yit nas the ground nat wounded with the plough,
But corn up-sprong, unsowe of mannes hond,
The which they gniden, and eete nat half y-nough.
No man yit knew the forwes of his lond;
No man the fyr out of the flint yit fond;
Un-korven and un-grobbed lay the vyne;
No man yit in the morter spyces grond
To clarre, ne to sause of galantyne.

No mader, welde, or wood no litestere
Ne knew; the flees was of his former hewe;
No flesh ne wiste offence of egge or spere;
No coyn ne knew man which was fals or trewe;

[30]

High in the trees, and all were eating,
And, in their manner, making feast;
In short there was so many a beast
That Algus, noble calculator,
Set in his counting-house to cater
For them, with all his figures ten
—For by those figures knowing men,
Can reckon, number and take count
Of all things to the right amount—
Would fail to reckon up the stream
Of wonders that I met in dream. . . .

2. *The Former Age*

A blissful life, a peaceable and sweet,
They led, those peoples in the former Age,
Contented with the fruit they found to eat
In fields, their customary heritage;
They were not spoilt or pampered into rage.
The quern was yet unknown, unknown the mill;
Beech-nuts they ate, and berries, and were sage,
And drank cold fountain-water from the hill.

Earth had not yet been wounded by the plough,
But corn sprang up, unseeded by man's hand;
They rubbed and ate—not half as much as now.
No one yet knew the furrows of his land,
Or had found fire in flint, I understand.
Vines lay ungrubbed, unpruned, nor were there seen
Mortars or pestles, spices were not planned
To sweeten wine or sauce a galantine.

Red madder, yellow weld (the dyer's care)
They knew not; fleeces kept their natural hue;
Flesh had no wound of sword or spear to bear,
There was no coinage, whether false or true;

No ship yit karf the wawes grene and blewe;
No marchaunt yit ne fette outlandish ware;
No trompes for the werres folk ne knewe,
No toures heye, and walles rounde or square.

What sholde it han avayled to werreye?
Ther lay no profit, ther was no richesse,
But cursed was the tyme, I dar wel seye,
That men first dide hir swety bysinesse
To grobbe up metal, lurkinge in darknesse,
And in the riveres first gemmes soghte.
Allas! than sprong up al the cursednesse
Of covetyse, that first our sorwe broghte!

Thise tyraunts putte hem gladly nat in pres,
No wildnesse, ne no busshes for to winne
Ther poverte is, as seith Diogenes,
Ther as vitaile is eek so skars and thinne
That noght but mast or apples is therinne.
But, ther as bagges been and fat vitaile,
Ther wol they gon, and spare for no sinne
With al hir ost the cite for t'assaile.

Yit were no paleis-chaumbres, ne non halles;
In caves and [in] wodes softe and swete
Slepten this blissed folk with-oute walles,
On gras or leves in parfit quiete.
No doun of fetheres, ne no bleched shete
Was kid to hem, but in seurtee they slepte;
Hir hertes were al oon, with-oute galles,
Everich of hem his feith to other kepte.

Unforged was the hauberk and the plate;
The lambish peple, voyd of alle vyce,
Hadden no fantasye to debate,
But ech of hem wolde other wel cheryce;
No pryde, non envye, non avaryce,
No lord, no taylage by no tyrannye;

No ship had carved the waters green and blue,
No merchant ferried home outlandish ware;
As yet no trumpet to the wars they knew,
No towers high, no bastions round or square.

What would it have availed them to make war?
No profit lay in that to fill the purse;
Cursed was the moment, that I'll answer for,
When they took on that sweaty job—and worse—
Grubbing up precious metals to imburse,
Or seeking gems on river-bed or reef;
From thence, alas, there sprang the human curse
Of covetous desire, that brought our grief.

These tyrants do not swell their armouries
A bush to gain, a wilderness to win;
They do not go (so says Diogenes)
Where men are poor and victuals scarce and thin
—Beech-nuts and mast, at best an apple-skin—
But where the big fat bags can be pulled down
They gladly go, and for no thought of sin
Will they hold back; their hosts assault the town.

There were no palace chambers then, no halls;
But there were caves in woodlands soft and sweet;
There slept those happy folk; protecting walls
They needed not, they lay in safe retreat
On grass or leaves; no down or laundered sheet
Was known to them; securely there they slept,
Their hearts at one—no bitterness or squalls;
And when they gave their word, their word was kept.

Unforged the hauberk and the armoured plate,
For the lamb-hearted peoples, void of vice,
Had then no furious fancies to debate,
And cherished one another at love's price;
No pride, no envy and no avarice,
No lord, no taxes raised by tyranny;

Humblesse and pees, good feith, the emperice,
[Fulfilled erthe of olde curtesye.]

Yit was not Jupiter the likerous,
That first was fader of delicacye,
Come in this world; ne Nembrot, desirous
To reynen, had nat maad his toures hye.
Allas, allas! now may men wepe and crye!
For in our dayes nis but covetyse
[And] doublenesse, and tresoun and envye,
Poysoun, manslauhtre, and mordre in sondry wyse.

3. *Troilus and Criseyde*

Book III, lines 1–49

O blisful light, of whiche the bemes clere
Adorneth al the thridde hevene faire!
O sonnes leef, O Joves doughter dere,
Plesaunce of love, O goodly debonaire.
In gentil hertes ay redy to repaire!
O verray cause of hele and of gladnesse,
Y-heried be thy might and thy goodnesse!

In hevene and helle, in erthe and salte see
Is felt thy might, if that I wel descerne;
As man, brid, best, fish, herbe and grene tree
Thee fele in tymes with vapour eterne.
God loveth, and to love wol nought werne;
And in this world no lyves creature,
With-outen love, is worth, or may endure.

Ye Joves first to thilke effectes glade,
Thorugh which that thinges liven alle and be,
Comeveden, and amorous him made
On mortal thing, and as yow list, ay ye

Peace, meekness and good faith, their Queen in this,
Filled the whole earth with ancient courtesy.

Not yet had Jupiter the Lecherous,
That first was father to foul luxuries,
Come to this world, nor Nimrod, furious
For power, had thrust his towers to the skies.
Well may we weep; alas for tears and cries!
For in our days there's nought but covetous minds,
Doubleness, treason, torture, envy, lies,
Manslaughter, poison, murders of all kinds.
(For David Cecil)

3. *Hymn to Heavenly Love*

O blissful light, whose beams in clearness run
Over all Third Heaven, adorning it with splendour,
O daughter of Jove and darling of the Sun,
Pleasure of Love! O affable and tender,
The ready guest of noble hearts, defender
And cause of all well-being and delight,
Worshipped be thy benignity and might!

In Heaven, in Hell, in earth and the salt sea,
Thy power is felt and is in evidence,
Since man, bird, beast, fish, herb and greening tree
Feel thee in season, eternal effluence!
God himself loves, nor turns his countenance thence,
And there's no creature in this world alive,
That without love has being, or can thrive.

Thou first didst move Jove to those glad effects
Through which it comes that all things live and are,
Madest him amorous, and, lo, he elects
His mortal loves; thou givest him, as far

Yeve him in love ese or adversitee;
And in a thousand formes doun him sente
For love in erthe, and whom yow liste, he hente.

Ye fierse Mars apeysen of his ire,
And, as yow list, ye maken hertes digne;
Algates, hem that ye wol sette a-fyre,
They dreden shame, and vices they resigne;
Ye do hem corteys be, fresshe and benigne,
And hye or lowe, after a wight entendeth;
The joyes that he hath, your might him sendeth.

Ye holden regne and hous in unitee;
Ye sooth fast cause of frendship been also;
Ye knowe al thilke covered qualitee
Of thinges which that folk on wondren so,
Whan they can not construe how it may jo,
She loveth him, or why he loveth here;
As why this fish, and nought that, cometh to were.

Ye folk a lawe han set in universe,
And this knowe I by hem that loveres be,
That who-so stryveth with yow hath the werse:
Now, lady bright, for thy benignitee,
At reverence of hem that serven thee,
Whos clerk I am, so techeth me devyse
Som joye of that is felt in thy servyse.

Ye in my naked herte sentement
Inhelde, and do me shewe of thy swetnesse.—
Caliope, thy vois be now present,
For now is nede; sestow not my destresse,
How I mot telle anon-right the gladnesse
Of Troilus, to Venus heryinge?
To which gladnes, who nede hath, god him bringe!

[36]

As pleases thee, his pleasure, or dost bar,
Sending him in a thousand shapes to look
For love on earth; and whom thou wouldst, he took.

Yes, and fierce Mars for thee has slaked his ire;
Thou canst ennoble every heart and face
As it may please thee; those thou wilt set on fire
Learn to dread shame and shun whatever is base.
Courteous thou makest them and fresh in grace;
And high or low, as his intent may be,
The joys a man may have are sent by thee.

Thou holdest realm and home in unity,
And art the steadfast cause of friendship too;
Thou knowest all the covered quality
Of things, that makes us wonder what or who
It is that makes them tick, and where's the clue
Why she loves him, or he loves there or here,
As why this fish, not that, comes to the weir.

Thy law is set upon the universe;
And this I know (for lovers told it me)
That he who strives against thee fares the worse.
Now, Lady bright, of thy benignity,
In reverence to those that worship thee,
Whose clerk I am, O teach me how to show
Some of the joy that, serving thee, they know!

Into my naked heart a sentience pour
With power to show thy sweetness and delight!
Caliope, be present! I implore
Thy voice, for now is need; thou seest my plight;
How shall I tell of Troilus' joy, or write
That all may honour Venus as they read it?
To all such joy may God bring those who need it!

4. *Troilus and Criseyde*

Book III, lines 50–168

Lay al this mene whyle Troilus,
Recordinge his lessoun in this manere,
'Ma fey!' thought he, 'thus wole I seye and thus;
Thus wole I pleyne un-to my lady dere;
That word is good, and this shal be my chere;
This nil I not foryeten in no wyse.'
God leve him werken as he gan devyse.

And lord, so that his herte gan to quappe,
Heringe hir come, and shorte for to syke!
And Pandarus, that ladde hir by the lappe,
Com neer, and gan in at the curtin pyke,
And seyde, 'god do bote on alle syke!
See, who is here yow comen to visyte;
Lo, here is she that is your deeth to wyte.'

Ther-with it semed as he wepte almost;
'A ha,' quod Troilus so rewfully,
'Wher me be wo, O mighty god, thou wost!
Who is al there? I see nought trewely.'
'Sire,' quod Criseyde, 'it is Pandare and I.'
'Ye, swete herte? allas, I may nought ryse
To knele, and do yow honour in som wyse.'

And dressede him upward, and she right tho
Gan bothe here hondes softe upon him leye,
'O, for the love of god, do ye not so

4. Troilus Declares his Love

(Sick with love's fever, Troilus lies in bed at the house of his brother, Deiphebus. Thither, by stratagem, his friend Pandarus has brought Criseyde (who is Pandarus' niece) in order to effect a first meeting between her and her lover, at which Troilus is to plead his love, for the first time in his life.)

He lay there all this meanwhile, Troilus,
Learning the lesson suited to his case;
'By Jove,' he thought, 'I shall say thus and thus,
And thus entreat my darling for her grace;
That's a good phrase! Thus I shall set my face;
This I must not forget.' Unhappy man!
Pray God all goes according to his plan!

Lord, how his heart began to quake and thrum,
Hearing her step! his sighs came short and thick;
Pandar had led her in, and then had come
Closer, and twitched the curtain, by a trick
To peep inside, and said 'God save the sick!
Just look who's come to see you! There she stands,
The one who has your murder on her hands.'

He spoke as if he were about to weep.
'Ah! Ah!' cried Troilus, with a pitiful sigh,
'God knows if I am ill! I cannot sleep,
I cannot see—who is it standing by?'
'Sir,' said Criseyde, 'it's Pandarus and I.'
'*You*, sweetheart? O alas I cannot kneel
Or rise, to show the reverence I feel.'

He raised himself a little, but she came
At once and softly laid her hand on his.
'You must not kneel to me! In heaven's name,

To me,' quod she, 'ey! what is this to seye?
Sire, come am I to yow for causes tweye;
First, yow to thonke, and of your lordshipe eke
Continuaunce I wolde yow biseke.'

This Troilus, that herde his lady preye
Of lordship him, wex neither quik ne deed,
Ne mighte a word for shame to it seye,
Al-though men sholde smyten of his heed.
But lord, so he wex sodeinliche reed,
And sire, his lesson, that he wende conne,
To preyen hir, is thurgh his wit y-ronne.

Criseyde al this aspyede wel y-nough,
For she was wys, and lovede him never-the-lasse,
Al nere he malapert, or made it tough,
Or was to bold, to singe a fool a masse.
But whan his shame gan somwhat to passe,
His resons, as I may my rymes holde,
I yow wol telle, as techen bokes olde

In chaunged vois, right for his verrey drede,
Which vois eek quook, and ther-to his manere
Goodly abayst, and now his hewes rede,
Now pale, un-to Criseyde, his lady dere,
With look doun cast and humble yolden chere,
Lo, th'alderfirste word that him asterte
Was, twyes, 'mercy, mercy, swete herte!'

And stinte a whyl, and whan he mighte out-bringe,
The nexte word was, 'god wot, for I have,
As feythfully as I have had konninge,
Ben youres, also god my sowle save;
And shal, til that I, woful wight, be grave.
And though I dar ne can un-to yow pleyne,
Y-wis, I suffre nought the lasse peyne.

What do you mean?' she said; 'two purposes
I have in coming, Sir; the first is this,
To thank you; next to beg continuance
Of your protection and your countenance.'

This Troilus, hearing his lady pray
For his support, felt neither quick nor dead;
Bashfulness left him not a word to say,
Not even if they'd come to take his head.
But, Lord! to see him suddenly turn red!
And, gentlemen, his lesson, learnt so neatly,
To beg her favour, disappeared completely.

All this Criseyde had noticed well enough,
For she was wise, and loved him never the less,
Though he was not self-confident or tough,
Nor tried to fool her with some fine address;
But what he said, as soon as his distress
Began to lessen, if my rhyme will hold,
I'll tell you, as my ancient author told.

In a changed voice, changed by his very dread,
Troilus answered in a manner bare
Of all assurance, and now blushing red,
Now paling, to Criseyde, his lady fair,
With downcast, humble and surrendered air,
Twice he burst forth; one word was all his art,
And it was 'Mercy! Mercy, sweetest heart!'

Silent a while, when he could speak again
The next word was 'God knows that when I gave
Myself to you, as far as it has lain
In me to do so, and as God may save
My soul, I became yours, and to the grave,
Poor wretch, shall be so; not that I complain
To you—but none the less I suffer pain.

Thus muche as now, O wommanliche wyf,
I may out-bringe, and if this yow displese,
That shal I wreke upon myn owne lyf
Right sone, I trowe, and doon your herte an ese,
If with my deeth your herte I may apese.
But sin that ye han herd me som-what seye,
Now recche I never how sone that I deye.'

Ther-with his manly sorwe to biholde,
It mighte han maad an herte of stoon to rewe;
And Pandare weep as he to watre wolde,
And poked ever his nece newe and newe,
And seyde, 'wo bigon ben hertes trewe!
For love of god, make of this thing an ende,
Or slee us bothe at ones, er that ye wende.'

'I? what?' quod she, 'by god and by my trouthe,
I noot nought what ye wilne that I seye.'
'I? what?' quod he, 'that ye han on him routhe,
For goddes love, and doth him nought to deye.'
'Now thanne thus,' quod she, 'I wolde him preye
To telle me the fyn of his entente;
Yet wiste I never wel what that he mente.'

'What that I mene, O swete herte dere?'
Quod Troilus, 'O goodly fresshe free!
That, with the stremes of your eyen clere,
Ye wolde som-tyme freendly on me see,
And thanne agreën that I may ben he,
With-oute braunche of vyce in any wyse,
In trouthe alwey to doon yow my servyse

As to my lady right and chief resort,
With al my wit and al my diligence,
And I to han, right as yow list, comfort,
Under your yerde, egal to myn offence,
As deeth, if that I breke your defence;

[42]

'This is as much, O sweet and womanly one,
As I may now bring forth; if this displease you,
I will revenge it on me and have done,
Soon, soon, and take my life, if that will ease you;
If with my death, indeed, I can appease you,
Since you have heard me speak at last, or try,
I do not care how soon I am to die.'

To see the manful sorrow that he felt
Might well have touched a heart of very stone;
Pandarus wept as if about to melt,
And nudged his niece anew at every moan;
'True are the hearts,' he said 'that weep alone!
O for the love of Heaven, end our woe,
Or kill us both together ere you go!'

'I . . ? What?' she said, 'By Heaven and in truth,
I've no idea what you would have me say.'
' "I . . ? What?" ' said he, have pity on his youth!
For God's love, would you have him pass away?'
'Well then,' she said, 'I'll ask him, if I may
What is the aim and end of his intent?
I never have truly gathered what he meant.'

'What I have meant? Ah, sweetest heart, my dear,'
Said Troilus, 'my lovely, fresh and free,
Let but the rivers of your eyes stream clear,
Once in a while, in friendliness on me,
And give me your consent I may be he
That, without any touch or vice, may ever
Offer his whole, true service and endeavour

'As to his lady and his chief resource,
With all my heart and mind and diligence,
And to be comforted, or feel the force
Of your displeasure, equal to my offence,
As death for any disobedience;

And that ye deigne me so muche honoure,
Me to comaunden ought in any houre.

And I to been your verray humble trewe,
Secret, and in my paynes pacient,
And ever-mo desire freshly newe,
To serven, and been y-lyke ay diligent,
And, with good herte, al holly your talent
Receyven wel, how sore that me smerte,
Lo, this mene I, myn owene swete herte.'

Quod Pandarus, 'lo, here an hard request,
And resonable, a lady for to werne!
Now, nece myn, by natal Joves fest,
Were I a god, ye sholde sterve as yerne,
That heren wel, this man wol no-thing yerne
But your honour, and seen him almost sterve,
And been so looth to suffren him yow serve.'

With that she gan hir eyen on him caste
Ful esily, and ful debonairly,
Avysing hir, and hyed not to faste
With never a word, but seyde him softely,
'Myn honour sauf, I wol wel trewely,
And in swich forme as he can now devyse,
Receyven him fully to my servyse,

Biseching him, for goddes love, that he
Wolde, in honour of trouthe and gentilesse,
As I wel mene, eek mene wel to me,
And myn honour, with wit and besinesse,
Ay kepe; and if I may don him gladnesse,
From hennes-forth, y-wis, I nil not feyne:
Now beeth al hool, no lenger ye ne pleyne.'

Deign me the honour, too, to use your power
Commanding me in all, at any hour,

'And I to be your ever-humble, true,
Secret in service, patient in distress,
And in desire constant, fresh and new
Servant, to serve you in all eagerness
In every inclination you express,
All it may cost accepting in good part,
See, that is what I mean, my sweetest heart.'

Said Pandarus 'Well! There's a hard request,
Reasonable for a lady to deny!
Now, little niece, by Jupiter the Blest,
Were I a god, you should be marked to die,
You, that can hear this man lay all else by
To guard your honour with a faith so fervent,
And yet are loth to take him for your servant!'

Now fully at her ease, she turned her eyes
To look at him, serenely debonair,
Thinking; she did not hurry her replies,
But in the end she answered him with care,
And softly said 'My honour safe and fair,
And in such form as you have heard him proffer,
I will receive his service, at his offer,

'Beseeching him, for Heaven's love, that he
Will, in all honour and without pretence,
As I mean well by him, mean well by me,
And guard my honour with all diligence.
If I can make him happy in this sense
Henceforward, then I will; this is no feigning;
And now be whole again, no more complaining.'

5. *The Knight's Tale*

lines 775–1746, with omissions

And on his hors, allone as he was born,
He carieth al this harneys him biforn;
And in the grove, at tyme and place y-set,
This Arcite and this Palamon ben met.
Tho chaungen gan the colour in hir face;
Right as the hunter in the regne of Trace,
That stondeth at the gappe with a spere,
Whan hunted is the leoun or the bere,
And hereth him come russhing in the greves,
And breketh bothe bowes and the leves,
And thinketh, 'heer cometh my mortel enemy,
With-oute faile, he moot be deed, or I;
For outher I mot sleen him at the gappe,
Or he mot sleen me, if that me mishappe:'
So ferden they, in chaunging of hir hewe,
As fer as everich of hem other knewe.
Ther nas no good day, ne no saluing;
But streight, with-outen word or rehersing,
Everich of hem halp for to armen other,
As freendly as he were his owne brother;
And after that, with sharpe speres stronge
They foynen ech at other wonder longe.
Thou mightest wene that this Palamoun
In his fighting were a wood leoun,
And as a cruel tygre was Arcite:
As wilde bores gonne they to smyte,
That frothen whyte as foom for ire wood.
Up to the ancle foghte they in hir blood.
And in this wyse I lete hem fighting dwelle
And forth I wol of Theseus yow telle.

   The destinee, ministre general,

5. *A Duel for Love*

Alone as at his birth Arcita rode
And carried all the amour in a load,
And in the grove, where time and place were set,
These two, Arcite and Palamon, are met.

  Then slowly changed the colour in each face,
Just as when hunters in the realm of Thrace,
Who, standing in the gap, will poise a spear
And wait for bear or lion to appear,
Then hear him coming, crashing through the branches,
And hear the swish of leaves upon his haunches,
And think 'Here comes my mortal enemy!
It's certain death for either him or me;
For either I must slay him in this gap,
Or he slay me, if I should have mishap.'
Just so these two changed colour as they met,
Knowing each other, and the purpose set.

  There was no salutation, no good day,
But without word or prelude, straight away,
Each of them gave his help to arm the other,
As friendly as if brother were arming brother,
And after that with spears of sharpened strength
They fought each other at amazing length.
You would have thought, seeing Palamon engage,
He was a lion, fighting-mad with rage,
Arcite a cruel tiger, as they beat
And smote each other; like wild boars that meet
And froth as white as foam upon the flood;
They fought till they were ankle-deep in blood,
And in this rage I leave them fighting thus
And turn once more to speak of Theseus.

  Now Destiny, that Minister General

That executeth in the world over-al
The purveyaunce, that God hath seyn biforn,
So strong it is, that, though the world had sworn
The contrarie of a thing, by ye or nay,
Yet somtyme it shal fallen on a day
That falleth nat eft with-inne a thousand yere.
For certeinly, our appetytes here,
Be it of werre, or pees, or hate, or love,
Al is this reuled by the sighte above.
This mene I now by mighty Theseus,
That for to honten is so desirous,
And namely at the grete hert in May,
That in his bed ther daweth him no day
That he nis clad, and redy for to ryde
With hunte and horn, and houndes him bisyde.
For in his hunting hath he swich delyt,
That it is al his joye and appetyt
To been him-self the grete hertes bane;
For after Mars he serveth now Diane.

 Cleer was the day, as I have told er this,
And Theseus, with alle joye and blis,
With his Ipolita, the fayre quene,
And Emelye, clothed al in grene,
On hunting be they riden royally.
And to the grove, that stood ful faste by,
In which ther was an hert, as men him tolde,
Duk Theseus the streighte wey hath holde.
And to the launde he rydeth him ful right,
For thider was the hert wont have his flight,
And over a brook, and so forth on his weye.
This duk wol han a cours at him, or tweye,
With houndes, swiche as that him list comaunde.

 And whan this duk was come un-to the launde,
Under the sonne he loketh, and anon
He was war of Arcite and Palamon,
That foughten breme, as it were bores two;
The brighte swerdes wenten to and fro
So hidously, that with the leeste strook

Who executes on earth and over all
What God from everlasting has foreseen,
Is of such strength, that though the world had been
Sure of the contrary by Yea and Nay,
That thing will happen on a certain day
Though never again within a thousand years.
And certainly our appetites and fears
Whether in war or peace, in hate or love,
Are governed by a Providence above.

This I apply to Theseus; every morn
He woke so eagerly for hound and horn,
Especially to hunt the hart in May,
That on his bed there never dawned a day
But he was up and ready dressed to ride,
With hound and horn and hunter at his side.
Hunting to him was such a keen delight,
It was his special joy and appetite
To be the stag's destroyer, for the stars
Ruled he should serve Diana after Mars.

Clear was the day, as I have told ere this,
And Theseus, in all jollity and bliss,
With fair Hippolyta, his lovely Queen,
And Emily, who was arrayed in green,
Rode out to hunt; it was a royal band;
And to the coppice lying near at hand
In which the hart—or so they told him—lay,
He led his gathering by the shortest way,
And, pressing on towards a glade in sight,
Down which the hart most often sped in flight,
Over a brook and off and out of view,
The Duke had planned to try a course or two
With certain hounds that he had singled out;
And when he reached the glade, he looked about.

Into the sun he looked, and thereupon
He saw Arcita fighting Palamon.
They fought like boars in bravery: there go
The shining swords in circle, to and fro,
So hideously that with the lightest stroke

It seemed as it wolde felle an ook;
But what they were, no-thing he ne woot.
This duk his courser with his spores smoot,
And at a stert he was bitwix hem two,
And pulled out a swerd and cryed, 'ho!
Namore, up peyne of lesing of your heed.
By mighty Mars, he shal anon be deed,
That smyteth any strook, that I may seen!
But telleth me what mister men ye been,
That been so hardy for to fighten here
With-outen juge or other officere,
As it were in a listes royally?'

This Palamon answerde hastily
And seyde: 'sire, what nedeth wordes mo?
We have the deeth deserved bothe two.
Two woful wrecches been we, two caytyves,
That been encombred of our owne lyves;
And as thou art a rightful lord and juge,
Ne yeve us neither mercy ne refuge,
But slee me first, for seynte charitee;
But slee my felawe eek as wel as me.
Or slee him first; for, though thou knowe it lyte,
This is thy mortal fo, this is Arcite,
That fro thy lond is banished on his heed,
For which he hath deserved to be deed.
And this is he that loveth Emelye.
For sith the day is come that I shal dye,
I make pleynly my confessioun,
That I am thilke woful Palamoun,
That hath thy prison broken wikkedly.
I am thy mortal fo, and it am I
That loveth so hote Emelye the brighte,
That I wol dye present in hir sighte.
Therfore I axe deeth and my juwyse;
But slee my felawe in the same wyse,
For bothe han we deserved to be slayn.'

This worthy duk answerde anon agayn,
And seyde, 'This is a short conclusioun:

It seemed as if they would have felled an oak.
Who they could be he did not know, of course,
But he clapped spur at once into his horse,
And at a bound he parted blow from blow
And, pulling out his sword, he shouted 'Ho!
No more on pain of death! Upon your head!
By might Mars, he is as good as dead
That dares to strike a blow in front of me!
Tell me what sort of fellows you may be
That have the impudence to combat here
Without a judge or other overseer,
Yet as if jousting at a royal tilt?'
Palamon answered quickly and with guilt
'O Sir, what need is there to waste my breath
In words? We both deserve to die the death
Two wretched men, your captives, met in strife,
And each of them encumbered with his life!
If to judge righteously has been your fashion,
Then show us neither mercy nor compassion,
And kill me first, for holy charity;
But kill my fellow too, as well as me;
Or kill him first, for little though you know,
This is Arcita and your mortal foe,
Banished by you on forfeit of his head,
For which alone he merits to be dead,
And it is he that loves my Emily;
Now, since my day of death has come to me,
I will make full confession, and go on
To say I am that woeful Palamon
Who broke out of your jail feloniously,
And it is I, your mortal enemy,
That am in love with Emily the bright,
Happy to die this moment in her sight.
And so I ask for judgment and for death,
But slay my fellow in the self-same breath,
Since we have both deserved that we be slain.'

And noble Theseus answered back again
'This is a short conclusion; it shall stand;

Youre owne mouth, by your confessioun,
Hath dampned you, and I wol it recorde,
It nedeth noght to pyne yow with the corde?

6. *The Knight's Tale*

lines 1625–1856, with omissions

Greet was the feste in Athenes that day,
And eek the lusty seson of that May
Made every wight to been in swich plesaunce,
That al that Monday justen they and daunce,
And spenden it in Venus heigh servyse.
But by the cause that they sholde ryse
Erly, for to seen the grete fight,
Unto hir reste wente they at night.
And on the morwe, whan that day gan springe,
Of hors and harneys, noyse and clateringe
Ther was in hostelryes al aboute;
And to the paleys rood ther many a route
Of lordes, up-on stedes and palfreys.
Ther maystow seen devysing of herneys
So uncouth and so riche, and wroght so weel
Of goldsmithrie, of browding, and of steel;
The sheeldes brighte, testers, and trappures;
Gold-hewen helmes, hauberks, cote-armures;
Lordes in paraments on hir courseres,
Knightes of retenue, and eek squyeres
Nailinge the speres, and helmes bokelinge,
Gigginge of sheeldes, with layneres lacinge;
Ther as need is, they weren no-thing ydel;
The fomy stedes on the golden brydel
Gnawinge, and faste the armurers also
With fyle and hamer prikinge to and fro;
Yemen on fote, and communes many oon
With shorte staves, thikke as they may goon;

Your own confession damns you out of hand;
I shall record your sentence as it stood;
There needs no torturing to make it good.'

6. *A Tournament for Love*

Great was the festival they held that day
In Athens, and the lusty time of May
Put everyone so well in countenance
They spent all Monday at a joust and dance
And the high services of Venus. Yet,
Because they knew that up they'd have to get,
And early too, to witness the great fight,
They went to bed betimes on Monday night.

  Next morning when the day began to spring
Clattering horse and noise of harnessing
Echoed through all the hostelries about.
Up to the palace cantered rout on rout
Of lords on palfreys, stallions, many a steed;
And what device of harness too indeed,
So rich and so outlandish, what a deal
Of goldsmith work, embroidery and steel!
Bright shields and trappings, headpieces and charms,
Great, golden helmets, hauberks, coats of arms,
Lords on apparelled coursers, squires too,
And knights belonging to their retinue,
Spears being nailed and helmets buckled strong,
Strappings of shields and lacing up of thong;
The work was urgent, not a man was idle.

  The foamy steeds gnawing the golden bridle,
The armourers up and down and roundabout,
Racing with file and hammer through the rout,
Yeomen on foot and commonalty come
With pipe and clarion, trump and kettle-drum,

Pypes, trompes, nakers, clariounes,
That in the bataille blowen blody sounes;
The paleys ful of peples up and doun,
Heer three, ther ten, holding hir questioun,
Divyninge of thise Theban knightes two.
Somme seyden thus, somme seyde it shal be so;
Somme helden with him with the blake berd,
Somme with the balled, somme with the thikke-herd;
Somme sayde, he loked grim and he wolde fighte;
He hath a sparth of twenty pound of wighte.
Thus was the halle ful of divyninge,
Longe after that the sonne gan to springe.

* * *

Up goon the trompes and the melodye.
And to the listes rit the companye
By ordinaunce, thurgh-out the citee large,
Hanged with cloth of gold, and nat with sarge.
Ful lyk a lord this noble duk gan ryde,
Thise two Thebanes up-on either syde;
And after rood the quene, and Emelye,
And after that another companye . . .
And west-ward, thurgh the gates under Marte,
Arcite, and eek the hundred of his parte,
With baner reed is entred right anon;
And in that selve moment Palamon
Is under Venus, est-ward in the place,
With baner whyt, and hardy chere and face. . . .
So even were they chosen, for to gesse.
And in two renges faire they hem dresse.
Whan that hir names rad were everichoon,
That in hir nombre gyle were ther noon,
Tho were the gates shet, and cryed was loude:
'Do now your devoir, yonge knightes proude!'

The heraudes lefte hir priking up and doun;
Now ringen trompes loude and clarioun;
Ther is namore to seyn, but west and est
In goon the speres ful sadly in arest;

Armed with short sticks, and making such a rattle,
It sounded like the blast of bloody battle.
The palace full of people up and down,
Here three, there ten, in all the talk of town,
And making bets about the Theban knights.
Says one 'He'll win!' Another 'Not by rights.'
Some backed a man whose beard was black and squared,
Some backed the skin-heads, some the shaggy-haired;
Said one 'There's a grim fellow! I'll be bound
He'll fight! His battle-axe weighs twenty pound.'
And prophecy went seething round the hall
Long after day had risen on them all.

* * *

Up go the trumpets and the melody,
Forth to the lists canter the company,
As they were bidden, to the city verge;
The streets were hung in cloth of gold, not serge.
And like a lord the Duke began to ride
With these two Theban knights on either side.
Behind them rode the Queen and Emily,
And behind them another company.
And westward, look! Under the Martian Gate,
Arcita and his hundred knights await,
And now, under a banner of red, march on;
And, at the self-same moment, Palamon
Enters by Venus' Gate and takes his place
Under a banner of white, with cheerful face.
They were so equal, one could only guess.

In two formations they began to dress,
And when the roll was called, that all might see
Their number was not swelled by treachery,
The gates were shut, and then the herald cried
'Young knights, now do your duty, show your pride.'

The heralds then withdrew, their work was done.
Out blared the trumpets and the clarion.
There is no more to say, but east and west
In go the spears in readiness, at the 'rest',

In goth the sharpe spore in-to the syde.
Ther seen men who can juste, and who can ryde;
Ther shiveren shaftes up-on sheeldes thikke;
He feleth thurgh the herte-spoon the prikke.
Up springen speres twenty foot on highte;
Out goon the swerdes as the silver brighte.
The helmes they to-hewen and to-shrede;
Out brest the blood, with sterne stremes rede.
With mighty maces the bones they to-breste.
He thurgh the thikkeste of the throng gan threste.
Ther stomblen stedes stronge, and doun goth al.
He rolleth under foot as dooth a bal.
He foyneth on his feet with his tronchoun,
And he him hurtleth with his hors adoun.
He thurgh the body is hurt, and sithen y-take,
Maugree his heed, and broght un-to the stake,
As forward was, right ther he moste abyde;
Another lad is on that other syde.
And som tyme dooth hem Theseus to reste,
Hem to refresshe, and drinken if hem leste.
Ful ofte a-day han thise Thebanes two
Togidre y-met, and wroght his felawe wo;
Unhorsed hath ech other of hem tweye.
Ther nas no tygre in the vale of Galgopheye,
Whan that hir whelp is stole, whan it is lyte,
So cruel on the hunte, as is Arcite
For jelous herte upon this Palamoun:
Ne in Belmarye ther nis so fel leoun,
That hunted is, or for his hunger wood,
Ne of his praye desireth so the blood,
As Palamon to sleen his fo Arcite.
The jelous strokes on hir helmes byte;
Out renneth blood on both hir sydes rede.

  Som tyme an ende ther is of every dede;
For er the sonne un-to the reste wente,
The stronge king Emetreus gan hente
This Palamon, as he faught with Arcite,
And made his swerd depe in his flesh to byte;

In go the spurs into the horses' side;
It's easy seeing who can joust and ride;
There the shafts shiver on the shields so thick,
One through his breast-bone feels the thrust and prick;
Up spring the spears to twenty foot in height,
Out come the long-swords, flashing silver-bright,
Hewing the helmets as they shear and shred,
Out bursts the blood in streams of sternest red,
The mighty maces swing, the bones are bashed,
One thrusting through the thickest throng has crashed,
There the strong steeds have stumbled, down goes all,
Man under foot, and rolling like a ball;
Another on his feet with truncheon pound
Hurtles a rider and his horse to ground;
One's wounded in the body, whom they take,
Spite of his teeth, and bear him to the stake,
As was ordained, and there he has to stay;
One more is carried off the other way.
From time to time the Duke decrees a rest,
To drink and be refreshed, as they think best.

  Many a time our Thebans in the flow
Of battle met, and did each other woe
And each unhorsed the other. There could be
No tiger in the Vale of Galgophy,
Raging in search after a stolen cub,
So cruel as Arcite with spear and club,
For jealousy of heart towards Palamon;
No lion could be so fierce to look upon
In all Benamarin, and none so savage
Being hunted, nor so hunger-mad in ravage
And thirst for blood, as Palamon for Arcite;
The blows upon their helmets bite and beat,
And the red blood runs out on man and steed.

  There comes an end at last to every deed,
And, ere into the west the sun had gone,
Strong King Emetrius took Palamon
As he was fighting with Arcite, still fresh,
And made his sword bite deeply in his flesh;

And by the force of twenty is he take
Unyolden, and y-drawe unto the stake.
And in the rescous of this Palamoun
The stronge king Ligurge is born adoun;
And king Emetreus, for al his strengthe,
Is born out of his sadel a swerdes lengthe,
So hitte him Palamon er he were take;
But al for noght, he was broght to the stake.
His hardy herte mighte him helpe naught;
He moste abyde, whan that he was caught
By force, and eek by composicioun.

Who sorweth now but woful Palamoun,
That moot namore goon agayn to fighte?
And whan that Theseus had seyn this sighte,
Un-to the folk that foghten thus echoon
He cryde, 'Ho! namore, for it is doon!
I wol be trewe juge, and no partye.
Arcite of Thebes shal have Emelye,
That by his fortune hath hir faire y-wonne.'
Anon ther is a noyse of peple bigonne
For joye of this, so loude and heigh with-alle,
It semed that the listes sholde falle.

The trompes, with the loude minstralcye,
The heraudes, that ful loude yolle and crye,
Been in hir wele for joye of daun Arcite.
But herkneth me, and stinteth now a lyte,
Which a miracle ther bifel anon.
This fierse Arcite hath of his helm y-don,
And on a courser, for to shewe his face,
He priketh endelong the large place,
Loking upward up-on this Emelye;
And she agayn him caste a freendlich yë,
(For wommen, as to speken in comune,
They folwen al the favour of fortune);
And she was al his chere, as in his herte.
Out of the ground a furie infernal sterte,
From Pluto sent, at requeste of Saturne,
For which his hors for fere gan to turne,

It asked the strength of twenty men to take
The yet-unyielded Palamon to stake.
Seeking a rescue, King Lycurgus coursed
Towards Palamon, but was himself unhorsed,
And King Emetrius, for all his strength,
Was flung out of his saddle a sword's length
By Palamon's last stroke in sweeping rake.
But all for nought, they brought him to the stake,
Nothing could help, however hard he fought,
His hardy heart must stay there, being caught
By force and by the rules decided on.
Who clamours now in grief but Palamon,
That may no more go in again and fight?

And when the noble Theseus saw this sight,
He rose and thundered forth to everyone
'Ho! Stop the fight! No more, for it is done.
I will be true judge and no partisan.
The Theban Prince Arcita is the man!
He shall have Emily, by Fortune's grace.'
A tumult of rejoicing filled all space
From every throat in such a caterwaul
It seemed as if the very lists would fall.

The trumpeters with loudest minstrelsy
And the shrill heralds, shouting frenziedly,
Were high in joy for honour of Arcite;
But wait a little, hear me, I repeat,
Look, what a miracle happened thereupon!
The fierce Arcita, with no helmet on,
Riding his courser round to show his face,
Cantered the whole length of the jousting place
Fixing his eye on Emily aloft
—And her returning gaze was sweet and soft,
For women, speaking generally, are prone
To follow Fortune's favours, once they're known—
She was his whole delight, his joy of heart.
Out of the ground behold a Fury start,
By Pluto sent, at the request of Saturn.
Arcita's horse in terror danced a pattern

And leep asyde, and foundred as he leep;
And, er that Arcite may taken keep,
He pighte him on the pomel of his heed,
That in the place he lay as he were deed,
His brest to-brosten with his sadel-bowe.
As blak he lay as any cole or crowe,
So was the blood y-ronnen in his face.
Anon he was y-born out of the place
With herte soor, to Theseus paleys.
Tho was he corven out of his harneys,
And in a bed y-brought ful faire and blyve,
For he was yet in memorie and alyve,
And alway crying after Emelye.

  Duk Theseus, with al his companye,
Is comen hoom to Athenes his citee,
With alle blisse and greet solempnitee.
Al be it that this aventure was falle,
He nolde noght disconforten hem alle.
Men seyde eek, that Arcite shal nat dye;
He shal ben heled of his maladye.
And of another thing they were as fayn,
That of hem alle was ther noon y-slayn,
Al were they sore y-hurt, and namely oon,
That with a spere was thirled his brest-boon.
To othere woundes, and to broken armes,
Some hadden salves, and some hadden charmes;
Fermacies of herbes, and eek save
They dronken, for they wolde hir limes have.

7. *Troilus and Criseyde*

Book III, lines 1184–1400

This Troilus, with blisse of that supprysed,
Put al in goddes hond, as he that mente
No-thing but wel; and, sodeynly avysed,

[60]

And leapt aside and foundered as he leapt,
And ere he was aware, Arcite was swept
Out of the saddle; he pitched upon his head
Onto the ground, and there he lay for dead;
His breast was shattered by the saddle-bow,
As black he lay as any coal or crow,
For all the blood had run into his face.
Immediately they bore him from the place,
Sadly, to Theseus' palace. What avail
Though he was carved out of his coat of mail
And put to bed with every care and skill?
Yet he was still alive, and conscious still,
And calling ceaselessly for Emily.
Theseus, attended by his company,
Came slowly home to Athens in full state
Of joyous festival, no less elate
For this misfortune, wishing not to cast
A gloom upon them all for what had passed.
Besides, they said Arcita would not die,
He would be healed, recovered, by and by.
And there was yet another thing that filled
All hearts with pleasure; no one had been killed,
Though some were badly hurt—among the rest
Especially the man with stoven chest.

As for the other wounds and broken arms
Some produced salves and some relied on charms;
He had a herb: there was a drug for him:
They drank them down and hoped to save a limb.

7. *A Consummation of Love*

This Troilus, by sudden bliss surprised,
Put all into God's hand, as one who meant
Nothing but well, and, suddenly advised

He hir in armes faste to him hente.
And Pandarus, with a ful good entente,
Leyde him to slepe, and seyde, 'if ye ben wyse,
Swowneth not now, lest more folk aryse.'

What mighte or may the sely larke seye,
Whan that the sparhauk hath it in his foot?
I can no more, but of thise ilke tweye,
To whom this tale sucre be or soot,
Though that I tarie a yeer, som-tyme I moot,
After myn auctor, tellen hir gladnesse,
As wel as I have told hir hevinesse.

Criseyde, which that felte hir thus y-take,
As writen clerkes in hir bokes olde,
Right as an aspes leef she gan to quake,
Whan she him felte hir in his armes folde.
But Troilus, al hool of cares colde,
Gan thanken tho the blisful goddes sevene;
Thus sondry peynes bringen folk to hevene.

This Troilus in armes gan hir streyne,
And seyde, 'O swete, as ever mote I goon,
Now be ye caught, now is ther but we tweyne;
Now yeldeth yow, for other boot is noon.'
To that Criseyde answerde thus anoon,
'Ne hadde I er now, my swete herte dere,
Ben yolde, y-wis, I were now not here!'

And as the newe abaysshed nightingale,
That stinteth first whan she biginneth singe,
Whan that she hereth any herde tale,
Or in the hegges any wight steringe,
And after siker dooth hir voys out-ringe;
Right so Criseyde, whan hir drede stente,
Opned hir herte, and tolde him hir entente.

By impulse, took her in his arms and bent
Her to him; Pandarus with kind intent
Went off to bed, saying 'If you are wise,
No fainting now, lest other people rise.'

What is there for the hapless lark to do
When taken in the sparrow-hawk's fierce foot?
There's nothing I can say; but of these two,
Whether you find my story sugar or soot,
I'd have to follow what my author put
Though I delayed a year, and to express
Their joy, as I have told their heaviness.

Criseyde, on feeling herself taken thus,
(As says my author in his ancient book)
In the enfolding arms of Troilus,
Lay trembling; like an aspen-leaf she shook.
And Troilus, with glory in his look,
Gave thanks to the bright gods and all their train;
So we may come to Paradise through pain.

Then Troilus who strained her as his own
Within his arms, whispered to her, to say
'Sweetest, are you not caught? We are alone;
Now yield yourself, there is no other way.'
And soon she answered him as there she lay
'Had I not yielded long ago, my dear,
My sweetest heart, I should not now be here.'

And as a nightingale that is abashed
And holds her peace, having begun to sing,
Because she may have heard the hedges crashed
By cattle, or the shout of shepherding,
Then, reassured, will let her music ring,
Just so, Criseyde, now that her fears were still,
Opened her heart to him and showed her will.

And right as he that seeth his deeth y-shapen,
And deye moot, in ought that he may gesse,
And sodeynly rescous doth him escapen,
And from his deeth is brought in sikernesse,
For al this world, in swich present gladnesse
Was Troilus, and hath his lady swete;
With worse hap god lat us never mete!

Hir armes smale, hir streyghte bak and softe,
Hir sydes longe, fleshly, smothe, and whyte
He gan to stroke, and good thrift bad ful ofte
Hir snowish throte, hir brestes rounde and lyte;
Thus in this hevene he gan him to delyte,
And ther-with-al a thousand tyme hir kiste;
That, what to done, for joye unnethe he wiste.

Than seyde he thus, 'O, Love, O, Charitee,
Thy moder eek, Citherea the swete,
After thy-self next heried be she,
Venus mene I, the wel-willy planete;
And next that, Imenëus, I thee grete;
For never man was to yow goddes holde
As I, which ye han brought fro cares colde.

Benigne Love, thou holy bond of thinges,
Who-so wol grace, and list thee nought honouren,
Lo, his desyr wol flee with-outen winges.
For, noldestow of bountee hem socouren
That serven best and most alwey labouren,
Yet were al lost, that dar I wel seyn, certes,
But-if they grace passed our desertes.

And therwith-al Criseyde anoon he kiste,
Of which, certeyn, she felte no disese.
And thus seyde he, 'now wolde god I wiste,
Myn herte swete, how I yow mighte plese!
What man,' quod he, 'was ever thus at ese
As I, on whiche the faireste and the beste
That ever I say, deyneth hir herte reste.

Like one who sees his death is taking shape,
And die he must, for all that he can see,
Whom suddenly a rescue and escape
Bring him from death to new security,
For all the world to such new ecstasy
With his sweet lady won, came Troilus;
God grant no worse a fortune fall to us!

Her delicate arms, her back so straight and soft,
Her slender flanks, flesh-soft and smooth and white
He then began to stroke, and blessed as oft
Her snowy throat, her breasts so round and slight,
And in this heaven taking his delight,
A thousand, thousand times he kissed her too,
For rapture scarcely knowing what to do.

And then he said 'O Love, O Charity,
Who, with thy Mother, Cytherea the Sweet,
After thyself is to be worshipped, she,
Venus, the planet of all kindly heat,
And next to you, Hymen I also greet,
For never to the gods was man beholden
As I, from cold care brought, to grace so golden.

'Benignest Love, thou holy bond of things,
Who seeks thy grace but renders thee no praise,
Lo! His desire would fly, but has no wings;
And were it not thy bounty deigns to raise
Those that best serve thee, labouring many days,
All would be lost; for what could they inherit
Unless thy grace were greater than their merit?'

And having spoken thus he kissed Criseyde,
At which she felt, be certain, no displeasure:
'Ah, would to God that I but knew,' he cried,
'How I might please you best, my heart, my treasure!
For was there ever man had such a measure
Of joy as I, on whom the loveliest
I ever saw has deigned her heart to rest?

And for the love of god, my lady dere,
Sin god hath wrought me for I shal yow serve,
As thus I mene, that ye wol be my stere,
To do me live, if that yow liste, or sterve,
So techeth me how that I may deserve
Your thank, so that I, thurgh myn ignoraunce,
Ne do no-thing that yow be displesaunce.

For certes, fresshe wommanliche wyf,
This dar I seye, that trouthe and diligence,
That shal ye finden in me al my lyf,
Ne I wol not, certeyn, breken your defence;
And if I do, present or in absence,
For love of god, lat slee me with the dede,
If that it lyke un-to your womanhede.'

'Y-wis,' quod she, 'myn owne hertes list,
My ground of ese, and al myn herte dere,
Graunt mercy, for on that is al my trist;
But late us falle awey from this matere;
For it suffyseth, this that seyd is here.
And at o word, with-outen repentaunce,
Wel-come, my knight, my pees, my suffisaunce!'

O blisful night, of hem so longe y-sought,
How blithe un-to hem bothe two thou were!
Why ne hadde I swich on with my soule y-bought,
Ye, or the leeste joye that was there?
A-wey, thou foule daunger and thou fere,
And lat hem in this hevene blisse dwelle,
That is so heygh, that al ne can I telle!

Thise ilke two, that ben in armes laft,
So looth to hem a-sonder goon it were,
That ech from other wende been biraft,
Or elles, lo, this was hir moste fere,
That al this thing but nyce dremes were;
For which ful ofte ech of hem seyde, 'O swete,
Clippe ich yow thus, or elles I it mete?'

'And, for the love of God, my lady dear,
Since He created me to serve your will,
—I mean it is His will that you should steer
My course of life, to save me or to kill—
Teach me to earn your thanks and to fulfill
Your wishes, so that I may never chance
On your displeasure, through my ignorance.

'O fresh and womanly love, I dare to give
This certain promise; truth and diligence,
These you will find in me, and while I live
I will be perfect in obedience;
And should I fail you, in presence or absence,
Let me be killed for it, if it seem good
To you, my darling, in your womanhood.'

'Indeed,' she said, 'dear heart of my desire,
Ground of my joy, my garner and my store,
I thank you for it with a trust entire
As it is thankful; let us say no more,
It is enough—for all was said before.
And, in a word that asks for no release,
Welcome my lover, my sufficing peace!'

O blissful night that they so long had sought,
How wert thou kindly to them both, how fair!
Would that my soul could such a night have bought,
Aye, or the least among the joys there were!
Away with coldness and away with care,
And in this bliss of heaven let them dwell,
Surpassing all that tongue of man can tell.

These very two in their embraces left,
So loath a moment to be disentwined,
Lest in their parting they should be bereft
Each of the other, or awake to find
It was a dream, a fancy of the mind,
Each to the other whispered in their kiss
'Can this be true? Or am I dreaming this?'

And, lord! so he gan goodly on hir see,
That never his look ne bleynte from hir face,
And seyde, 'O dere herte, may it be
That it be sooth, that ye ben in this place?'
'Ye, herte myn, god thank I of his grace!'
Quod tho Criseyde, and therwith-al him kiste,
That where his spirit was, for joye he niste.

This Troilus ful ofte hir eyen two
Gan for to kisse, and seyde, 'O eyen clere,
It were ye that wroughte me swich wo,
Ye humble nettes of my lady dere!
Though ther be mercy writen in your chere,
God wot, the text ful hard is, sooth, to finde,
How coude ye with-outen bond me binde?'

Therwith he gan hir faste in armes take,
And wel an hundred tymes gan he syke,
Nought swiche sorwful sykes as men make
For wo, or elles whan that folk ben syke,
But esy sykes, swiche as been to lyke,
That shewed his affeccioun with-inne;
Of swiche sykes coude he nought bilinne.

Sone after this they speke of sondry thinges,
As fil to purpos of this aventure,
And pleyinge entrechaungeden hir ringes,
Of which I can nought tellen no scripture;
But wel I woot a broche, gold and asure,
In whiche a ruby set was lyk an herte,
Criseyde him yaf, and stak it on his sherte.

Thise ilke two, of whom that I yow seye,
Whan that hir hertes wel assured were,
Tho gonne they to speken and to pleye,
And eek rehercen how, and whanne, and where,
They knewe hem first, and every wo and fere
That passed was; but al swich hevinesse,
I thanke it god, was tourned to gladnesse.

Lord, how he gazed at her, how blissfully!
His hungry eyes now never left her face,
And still he said 'Dear heart, O can it be
That you are truly in this very place?'
'Yes, yes, indeed I am, by heaven's grace'
Criseyde gave answer with so soft a kiss
His spirit knew not where it was, for bliss.

With many kisses Troilus again
Touching her fluttered eyelids, made reply
'Clear eyes, you were the cause of all my pain,
The humble nets my lady caught me by!
Though mercy may be written in her eye,
God knows the text was difficult to find;
How was I bound, without a thong to bind?'

Then in his arms he took and held her close
And sighs welled up in him and took their flight
A hundred times, nor were they such as those
Men sigh in grief or sickness, but the right
And easy sighs of passion and delight,
Sighs on the quickening pulse of love within,
That none will wish away when they begin.

Soon after this they spoke of many things,
Seeking their great adventure to unfold,
And made a playful interchange of rings
(Though what the posy was we are not told)
Yet, well I know, there was a brooch of gold
And blue, set with a ruby heart, she took
And pinned upon his shirt—so says the book.

These very two whose tale I have to tell,
Deep in the new assurance that was theirs,
Played in their talk and found it joy to dwell
On every detail, all the whens and wheres
And hows of their first meetings, and the cares
That now were passed, their heavy hearts, their sadness,
Which, I thank God, had all been turned to gladness.

8. *The Wife of Bath's Tale*

lines 253–308, with omissions

But for ye speken of swich gentillesse
As is descended out of old richesse,
That therfore sholden ye be gentil men,
Swich arrogance is nat worth an hen.
Loke who that is most vertuous alway,
Privee and apert, and most entendeth ay
To do the gentil dedes that he can,
And tak him for the grettest gentil man.
Crist wol, we clayme of him our gentillesse,
Nat of our eldres for hir old richesse.
For thogh they yeve us al hir heritage,
For which we clayme to been of heigh parage,
Yet may they nat biquethe, for no-thing,
To noon of us hir vertuous living,
That made hem gentil men y-called be;
And bad us folwen hem in swich degree.

Wel can the wyse poete of Florence,
That highte Dant, speken in this sentence;
Lo in swich maner rym is Dantes tale:
'Ful selde up ryseth by his branches smale
Prowesse of man; for god, of his goodnesse,
Wol that of him we clayme our gentillesse;'
For of our eldres may we no-thing clayme
But temporel thing, that man may hurte and mayme.

Eek every wight wot this as wel as I,
If gentillesse were planted naturelly
Un-to a certeyn linage, doun the lyne,
Privee ne apert, than wolde they never fyne
To doon of gentillesse the faire offyce;
They mighte do no vileinye or vyce.

Tak fyr, and ber it in the derkeste hous

8. *The Idea of a Gentleman*

But, since you spoke to me of gentle birth,
Such as descends from ancient wealth and worth,
By which you claim that you are gentlemen,
That is mere arrogance, not worth a hen.
Whoever gives himself to virtuous ends,
Private or public, and who most intends
To do what deeds of gentleness he can,
Take him to be the greatest gentleman.
Christ wills we claim our gentleness from Him,
Not from a wealth of ancestry long dim,
Though they bequeath their whole establishment
By which we claim to be of high descent,
Our fathers cannot make us a bequest
Of the fair vertues that became them best,
And earned for them the name of gentleman
And bade us follow them as best we can.

   Thus the wise poet of the Florentines
Whose name was Dante tells us, in these lines,
(Yes, this is the opinion Dante launches)
'Seldom arises by these slender branches
Prowess of men, for it is God, no less,
Who wills we claim of Him our gentleness,'
For, of our parents, nothing can we claim,
Save temporal things, and these may hurt and maim . . .

   But everyone knows this as well as I;
For if true gentleness were planted by
Natural inheritance all down the line,
It openly and secretly would shine,
And never cease to do its noble task;
How could they then do villainy, I ask?

   Take fire and carry it to the darkest house

Bitwix this and the mount of Caucasus,
And lat men shette the dores and go thenne;
Yet wol the fyr as faire lye and brenne,
As twenty thousand men mighte it biholde;
His office naturel ay wol it holde,
Up peril of my lyf, til that it dye.

Heer may ye see wel, how that genterye
Is nat annexed to possessioun,
Sith folk ne doon hir operacioun
Alwey, as dooth the fyr, lo! in his kinde.
For, god it woot, men may wel often finde
A lordes sone do shame and vileinye;
And he that wol han prys of his gentrye
For he was boren of a gentil hous,
And hadde hise eldres noble and vertuous,
And nil him-selven do no gentil dedis,
Ne folwe his gentil auncestre that deed is,
He nis nat gentil, be he duk or erl;
For vileyns sinful dedes make a cherl.
For gentillesse nis but renomee
Of thyne auncestres, for hir heigh bountee,
Which is a strange thing to thy persone.
Thy gentillesse cometh fro god allone;
Than comth our verray gentillesse of grace,
It was no-thing biquethe us with our place.

Between this kingdom and the Caucasus,
And shut the doors on it and leave it there,
It will burn on, and it will burn as fair
As if ten thousand men were there to see;
For fire will keep its nature and degree,
On peril of my life, until it dies;
But gentleness, as you must recognise,
Is not annexed in Nature to possessions;
Men fail in living up to their professions,
But fire never ceases to be fire.
God knows you'll often find, if you enquire,
Some lording doing villainy and shame.
If you would be esteemed for the mere name
Of having been born into a noble house,
Of parents virtuous and generous,
And do not live to do a gentle deed,
Or follow your dead father's noble creed,
You are no gentleman, though Duke or Earl.
It's sin and villainy that make a churl.
Gentility is only the renown
For bounty that your fathers handed down,
And foreign to your person, not your own;
A noble nature comes from God alone;
Our gentleness comes to us, then, by grace,
Not by inheritance of rank or place.

9. The Franklin's Tale

lines 511–896, with omissions

Arveragus and Dorigen are lovers who have married on the understanding that he will continue to obey her, as a lover obeys his mistress, instead of commanding her, as a husband commands his wife, except of course in public, when it is as much in her interests as his that he should seem to retain the honour of his rank and authority. The bargain works perfectly, their love continues in a happy marriage; after a few years Arveragus goes abroad from Brittany to England for a Tournament in which he wishes to show his prowess; Dorigen, disconsolate, can only think of the terrible rocks of Brittany on which he may be wrecked as he returns. To cheer her up, her friends get up a party. At the party there appears a young man called Aurelius, who has been secretly in love with Dorigen for a long time. He declares his love to her

> Upon the morwe, whan that it was day,
> To Britaigne toke they the righte way,
> Aurelius, and this magicien bisyde,
> And been descended ther they wolde abyde;
> And this was, as the bokes me remembre,
> The colde frosty seson of Decembre.
>
> Phebus wex old, and hewed lyk latoun,
> That in his hote declinacioun
> Shoon as the burned gold with stremes brighte;
> But now in Capricorn adoun he lighte,
> Wher-as he shoon ful pale, I dar wel seyn.
> The bittre frostes, with the sleet and reyn,
> Destroyed hath the grene in every yerd.
> Janus sit by the fyr, with double berd,
> And drinketh of his bugle-horn the wyn.
> Biforn him stant braun of the tusked swyn,
> And 'Nowel' cryeth every lusty man.
>
> Aurelius, in al that ever he can,
> Doth to his maister chere and reverence,

9. Which Behaved Best?

and begs for hers in return. She is at first outraged by the suggestion, rebukes him, and repulses him, but, seeing his misery, she relents so far as to offer, almost as a jest, to yield to his desires, provided that he will first remove the rocks of Brittany, which she supposes to be an impossibility. Aurelius goes off in despair and takes to his bed, sick for love. But his brother suddenly remembers that there is such a thing as Magic, and he recalls a Philosopher-Magician he had once known at Orleans, who might be worth consulting. Aurelius and his brother go off at once to Orleans, meet the Philosopher-Magician, and put their problem to him. After some talk, he agrees to remove the rocks of Brittany, or at least to create the illusion that they have been removed, but says his fee is a thousand pounds. Aurelius jumps at the offer and the bargain is struck:

> And morning came; as soon as it was day,
> They made for Brittany by the nearest way,
> These brothers, with the wizard at their side,
> And there dismounted, having done their ride.
> It was—so say the books, as I remember,
> The cold and frosty season of December.
> Phoebus grew old, his coppery face was duller
> Than it had been in *Cancer*, when his colour
> Shone with the burnished gold of streaming morn,
> But now, declining down in *Capricorn*,
> His face shone very pale, I dare maintain.
> The bitter frosts, the driving sleet and rain,
> Had killed the gardens; greens had disappeared;
> Now Janus by the fire, with double-beard,
> His bugle-horn in hand, sits drinking wine;
> Before him stands a brawn of tusky swine,
> And '*Sing Noel*' cries every lusty man.
> Aurelius, using all the means he can,
> Gives welcome to the Master, shows respect,

And preyeth him to doon his diligence
To bringen him out of his peynes smerte,
Or with a swerd that he wolde slitte his herte.

   This subtil clerk swich routhe had of this man,
That night and day he spedde him that he can,
To wayte a tyme of his conclusioun;
This is to seye, to make illusioun,
By swich an apparence or jogelrye,
I ne can no termes of astrologye,
That she and every wight sholde wene and seye,
That of Britaigne the rokkes were aweye,
Or elles they were sonken under grounde.
So atte laste he hath his tyme y-founde
To maken his japes and his wrecchednesse
Of swich a supersticious cursednesse.
His tables Toletanes forth he broght,
Ful wel corrected, ne ther lakked noght,
Neither his collect ne his expans yeres,
Ne his rotes ne his othere geres,
And knew also his othere observaunces
For swiche illusiouns and swiche meschaunces
As hethen folk used in thilke dayes;
For which no lenger maked he delayes,
But thurgh his magik, for a wyke or tweye,
It semed that alle the rokkes were aweye.

   Aurelius, which that yet despeired is
Wher he shal han his love or fare amis,
Awaiteth night and day on this miracle;
And whan he knew that ther was noon obstacle,
That voided were thise rokkes everichon,
Doun to his maistres feet he fil anon,
And seyde, 'I woful wrecche, Aurelius,
Thanke yow, lord, and lady myn Venus,
That me han holpen fro my cares colde:'
And to the temple his wey forth hath he holde,
Wher-as he knew he sholde his lady see.

And begs his diligence, that no neglect,
Or sloth delay the healing of his smart,
Or he would take a sword and pierce his heart.

  The subtle sage had pity on the man,
So night and day went forward with his plan,
Watching the hour to favour the conclusion
Of his experiment, that by illusion,
Or apparition—call it jugglery,
I lack the jargon of astrology—
When she and all the world would think and say
The rocks of Brittany had gone away,
Or else that they had sunk under the ground.
And so the favouring hour at last was found
To do his tricks—the wretched exhibition
Of that abominable superstition.

  His calculating tables were brought out,
Newly corrected (he made sure about
The years in series and the single years
To fix the points the planets in their spheres
Were due to reach, and so assessed their 'root'
In Longitude) and other things to suit,
With all the relevant arithmetic
For his illusion, for the wretched trick
He meant to play, as, in those heathen days,
People would do. There were no more delays
And, by his magic, for a week or more,
It seemed the rocks had gone; he'd cleared the shore.

  Aurelius still in his despair and doubt
—Was he to have his love, or do without?—
Watched for this miracle by day and night
And when he saw no obstacle in sight,
The rocks all voided and the work complete,
He fell in rapture at his Master's feet,
'Wretch as I am, for what has passed between us,'
He said 'to you and to my Lady Venus,
I offer thanks, that saved me from cold care.'
He took his way then to the temple there,
Where, as he knew, his lady was to be;

And whan he saugh his tyme, anon-right he,
With dredful herte and with ful humble chere,
Salewed hath his sovereyn lady dere:
　'My righte lady,' quod this woful man,
'Whom I most drede and love as I best can,
And lothest were of al this world displese,
Nere it that I for yow have swich disese,
That I moste dyen heer at your foot anon,
Noght wolde I telle how me is wo bigon;
But certes outher moste I dye or pleyne;
Ye slee me giltelees for verray peyne.
But of my deeth, thogh that ye have no routhe,
Avyseth yow, er that ye breke your trouthe.
Repenteth yow, for thilke god above,
Er ye me sleen by-cause that I yow love.
For, madame, wel ye woot what ye han hight;
Nat that I chalange any thing of right
Of yow my sovereyn lady, but your grace;
But in a gardin yond, at swich a place,
Ye woot right wel what ye bihighten me;
And in myn hand your trouthe plighten ye
To love me best, god woot, ye seyde so,
Al be that I unworthy be therto.
Madame, I speke it for the honour of yow,
More than to save myn hertes lyf right now;
I have do so as ye comanded me;
And if ye vouche-sauf, ye may go see.
Doth as yow list, have your biheste in minde,
For quik or deed, right ther ye shul me finde;
In yow lyth al, to do me live or deye;—
But wel I woot the rokkes been aweye!'

　He taketh his leve, and she astonied stood,
In al hir face nas a drope of blood;
She wende never han come in swich a trappe:
'Allas!' quod she, 'that ever this sholde happe!
For wende I never, by possibilitee,
That swich a monstre or merveille mighte be!
It is agayns the proces of nature:'

And when he saw his opportunity,
With quaking heart and with a humble face
He made obeisance to her sovereign grace.

'My own, true lady,' said this woeful man,
'Whom most I dread and love, as best I can,
Last in the world of those I would displease,
Had I not had so many miseries
That I might die, here, at your very feet,
I would not tell you what I suffer, sweet,
But either I must die, or make lament;
Truly the pain is killing me, innocent.
But though my death could never so have stirred
Your pity, think before you break your word.
Repent it, for the love of God above you,
Before you murder me because I love you!
You well know what you promised to requite
—Not that I challenge anything of right,
But only, sovereign lady, of your grace;
Yet in that garden, and at such a place,
You know right well the vow you made to me,
Your plighted truth into my hand,' said he,
'To love me best, you said, as God above
Well knows, although unworthy of your love.
Madam, it is your honour that I seek
More than to save my life, in what I speak.
I have performed what you commanded me,
As, if you deign to look, you well may see.
Do as you please, but think of what you said,
For you will find me here, alive or dead;
It lies in you to save me or to slay,
But well I know the rocks are all away!'

He took his leave; she, rooted to the place,
Without a drop of colour in her face,
Stood there astonished at her strange mishap;
'Alas!' she said, 'to fall in such a trap!
I never thought the possibility
Of such a monstrous miracle could be!
It goes against the processes of nature.'

And hoom she gooth a sorweful creature.
For verray fere unnethe may she go,
She wepeth, wailleth, al a day or two,

   But nathelees, upon the thridde night,
Hom cam Arveragus, this worthy knight,
And asked hir, why that she weep so sore?
And she gan wepen ever lenger the more.

   'Allas!' quod she, 'that ever was I born!
Thus have I seyd,' quod she, 'thus have I sworn'—
And told him al as ye han herd bifore;
It nedeth nat reherce it yow na-more.

   This housbond with glad chere, in freendly wyse,
Answerde and seyde as I shal yow devyse:
'Is ther oght elles, Dorigen, but this?'

   'Nay, nay,' quod she, 'god help me so, as wis;
This is to muche, and it were goddes wille.'

   'Ye, wyf,' quod he, 'lat slepen that is stille;
It may be wel, paraventure, yet to-day.
Ye shul your trouthe holden, by my fay!
For god so wisly have mercy on me,
I hadde wel lever y-stiked for to be,
For verray love which that I to yow have,
But-if ye sholde your trouthe kepe and save.
Trouthe is the hyeste thing that man may kepe:'—
But with that word he brast anon to wepe,
And seyde, 'I yow forbede, up peyne of deeth,
That never, whyl thee lasteth lyf ne breeth,
To no wight tel thou of this aventure.
As I may best, I wol my wo endure,
Ne make no contenance of hevinesse,
That folk of yow may demen harm or gesse.'

   And forth he cleped a squyer and a mayde:
'Goth forth anon with Dorigen,' he sayde,
'And bringeth hir to swich a place anon.'
They take hir leve, and on hir wey they gon;
But they ne wiste why she thider wente.
He nolde no wight tellen his entente.

   Paraventure an heep of yow, y-wis,

And home she went, a very sorrowful creature,
In very fear, and she had much to do
Even to walk; she wept a day or two.
  On the third day, however, of her plight,
Home came Arveragus, that excellent knight,
And questioned her; what was she crying for?
But she continued weeping all the more.
'Alas!' said she 'that ever I was born!
Thus have I said,' she answered, 'thus have sworn!'
She told him all, as you have heard before,
Why then repeat it to you all once more?
Her husband smiled and in a friendly way
Made answer to her then, as I shall say:
'And is there nothing, Dorigen, but this?'
'No, no, so help me God! But what's amiss
Is much—too much, although it were God's will.'
'Well, wife,' said he, 'let sleeping dogs lie still;
All may perhaps be well, this very day;
But you shall keep your word to him, I say,
For, as may God be merciful to me,
I rather would be stabbed to death' said he,
For very love of you, since you have spoken,
Than you should fail to keep your truth unbroken,
Truth is the highest thing in a man's keeping.'
But with that word he suddenly burst out weeping,
And said 'But I forbid you, on pain of death,
As long as life may last and you draw breath,
Ever to speak a word of this affair
To anyone; and what I have to bear
I'll bear as best I may; now clear your face,
That nobody may guess at this disgrace.'
  He called a maidservant and squire then
And said 'Go out with Lady Dorigen,
To such and such a place,' and, being sent,
They took their leave of him and off they went,
But did not know what reason lay behind;
He would tell no one what was in his mind.
  Perhaps a heap of you will want to say

Wol holden him a lewed man in this,
That he wol putte his wyf in jupartye;
Herkneth the tale, er ye up-on hir crye.
She may have bettre fortune than yow semeth;
And whan that ye han herd the tale, demeth.

    This squyer, which that highte Aurelius,
On Dorigen that was so amorous,
Of aventure happed hir to mete
Amidde the toun, right in the quikkest strete,
As she was boun to goon the wey forthright
Toward the gardin ther-as she had hight.
And he was to the gardinward also;
For wel he spyed, whan she wolde go
Out of hir hous to any maner place.
But thus they mette, of aventure or grace;
And he saleweth hir with glad entente,
And asked of hir whiderward she wente?

    And she answerde, half as she were mad,
'Un-to the gardin, as myn housbond bad,
My trouthe for to holde, allas! allas!'

    Aurelius gan wondren on this cas,
And in his herte had greet compassioun
Of hir and of hir lamentacioun,
And of Arveragus, the worthy knight,
That bad hir holden al that she had hight,
So looth him was his wyf sholde breke hir trouthe;
And in his herte he caughte of this greet routhe,
Consideringe the beste on every syde,
That fro his lust yet were him lever abyde
Than doon so heigh a cherlish wrecchednesse
Agayns franchyse and alle gentillesse;
For which in fewe wordes seyde he thus:

    'Madame, seyth to your lord Arveragus,
That sith I see his grete gentillesse
To yow, and eek I see wel your distresse,
That him were lever han shame (and that were routhe)
Than ye to me sholde breke thus your trouthe,
I have wel lever ever to suffre wo

He was a lout to act in such a way,
Putting his wife into such jeopardy!
Listen before you judge them; wait and see.
She may have better luck than you suppose;
Judge when you've heard the story to its close.

　Now to Aurelius let us turn again,
This squire so in love with Dorigen;
By accident they happened soon to meet
Near the town centre, in the busiest street,
Which she was bound to use, however loath,
To reach the garden and to keep her oath.
Aurelius gardenwards was going too;
A faithful spy on all she used to do,
He kept close watch whenever she went out,
And so by accident, or luck, no doubt,
They met each other; with his features glowing
With happiness, he asked where she was going?
And she replied, as one half driven mad,
Why, to the garden, as my husband bad,
To keep my plighted word, alas, alas!'

　Aurelius, stunned at what had come to pass,
Felt a great surge of pity that arose
At sight of her, lamenting in her woes,
And for Arveragus, that noble knight
That bade her keep her word of honour white,
So loath he was that she should break her truth.
And such a rush of pity filled the youth
That he was moved to think the better course
Was to forgo his passion than to force
An act on her, of gross and churlish kind,
And against such nobility of mind;
So, in few words, the lad addressed her thus:

　'Madam, say to your lord, Arveragus,
That since I well perceive his nobleness
Towards you, and I see your own distress,
Knowing the shame that he would rather take
(And that were pity) than that you should break
Your plighted word, I'd rather suffer too

Than I departe the love bitwix yow two.
I yow relesse, madame, in-to your hond
Quit every surement and every bond,
That ye han maad to me as heer-biforn,
Sith thilke tyme which that ye were born.
My trouthe I plighte, I shal yow never repreve
Of no biheste, and here I take my leve,
As of the treweste and the beste wyf
That ever yet I knew in al my lyf.
But every wyf be-war of hir biheste,
On Dorigene remembreth atte leste.
Thus can a squyer doon a gentil dede,
As well as can a knight, with-outen drede.'

   She thonketh him up-on hir knees al bare,
And hoom un-to hir housbond is she fare,
And tolde him al as ye han herd me sayd;
And be ye siker, he was so weel apayd,
That it were inpossible me to wryte;
What sholde I lenger of this cas endyte?

   Arveragus and Dorigene his wyf
In sovereyn blisse leden forth hir lyf.
Never eft ne was ther angre hem bitwene;
He cherisseth hir as though she were a quene;
And she was to him trewe for evermore.
Of thise two folk ye gete of me na-more.

   Aurelius, that his cost hath al forlorn,
Curseth the tyme that ever he was born:
'Allas,' quod he, 'allas! that I bihighte
Of pured gold a thousand pound of wighte
Un-to this philosophre! how shal I do?
I see na-more but that I am fordo.
Myn heritage moot I nedes selle,
And been a begger; heer may I nat dwelle,
And shamen al my kinrede in this place,
But I of him may gete bettre grace.
But nathelees, I wol of him assaye,
At certeyn dayes, yeer by yeer, to paye,
And thanke him of his grete curteisye;

For ever, than come between his love and you;
  'So, Madam, I release into your hand
All bonds or deeds of covenant that stand
Between us, and suppose all treaties torn
You may have made with me since you were born.
I give my word never to chide or grieve you
For any promise given, and so I leave you,
Madam, the very best and truest wife,
That ever yet I knew in all my life.
Women, beware of what you promise men,
Or, at the least, remember Dorigen!
A squire can do a generous thing with grace,
As well as can a knight, in any case.'
  And she went down and thanked him on her knees.
Home to her husband then, with heart at ease,
She went and told him all, as I've recorded;
You may be sure he felt so well rewarded
No words of mine could possibly express
His feelings; therefore, of his happiness
I will not speak; with Dorigen, his wife,
In sovereign bliss thereafter, he led his life,
No anger in their love was ever seen;
He cherished her as though she were a queen,
She stayed as true as she had been before;
Of these two lovers you will get no more.

  Aurelius, all whose labour had been lost,
Cursing his birth, reflected on the cost.
'Alas!' he said 'alas, that I am bound
To pay in solid gold a thousand pound
To this philosopher! What shall I do?
All I can see is that I'm ruined too;
There's my inheritance; I'll have to sell,
And be a beggar; here I cannot dwell,
I cannot be a shame and a disgrace
To all my family; I must leave the place,
Unless he shows some mercy; I could pay
A yearly sum upon a certain day,
And thank him gratefully; I can but try;

My trouthe wol I kepe, I wol nat lye.'
   With herte soor he gooth un-to his cofre,
And broghte gold un-to this philosophre,
The value of fyve hundred pound, I gesse,
And him bisecheth, of his gentillesse,
To graunte him dayes of the remenaunt,
And seyde, 'maister, I dar wel make avaunt,
I failled never of my trouthe as yit;
For sikerly my dette shal be quit
Towardes yow, how-ever that I fare
To goon a-begged in my kirtle bare.
But wolde ye vouche-sauf, up-on seurtee,
Two yeer or three for to respyten me,
Than were I wel; for elles moot I selle
Myn heritage; ther is na-more to telle.'
   This philosophre sobrely answerde,
And seyde thus, whan he thise wordes herde:
'Have I nat holden covenant un-to thee?'
'Yes, certes, wel and trewely,' quod he.
'Hastow nat had thy lady as thee lyketh?'
'No, no,' quod he, and sorwefully he syketh.
'What was the cause? tel me if thou can.'
Aurelius his tale anon bigan,
And tolde him al, as ye han herd bifore;
It nedeth nat to yow reherce it more.
   He seide, 'Arveragus, of gentillesse,
Had lever dye in sorwe and in distresse
Than that his wyf were of hir trouthe fals.'
The sorwe of Dorigen he tolde him als,
How looth hir was to been a wikked wyf,
And that she lever had lost that day hir lyf,
And that hir trouthe she swoor, thurgh innocence:
'She never erst herde speke of apparence;
That made me han of hir so greet pitee.
And right as frely as he sente hir me,
As frely sente I hir to him ageyn.
This al and som, ther is na-more to seyn.'
   This philosophre answerde, 'leve brother,

But I will keep my truth, I will not lie.'
    And sad at heart he went to search his coffer
And gathered up what gold he had to offer
His Master—some five hundred pounds, I guess—
And begged him as a gentleman, no less,
To grant him time enough to pay the rest.
    'Sir, I can boast, in making this request,
He said, 'I never failed my word as yet
And I will certainly repay this debt
I owe you, sir, however it may hurt,
Though I should go a-begging in my shirt.
If you would grant me, on security,
A little respite, say, two years or three,
All would be fine; if not, I'll have to sell
My patrimony; there's no more to tell.'
    Then this philosopher, in sober pride,
Having considered what he'd said, replied
'Did I not keep my covenant with you?'
'You did indeed' he said, 'and truly too.'
'And did you not enjoy your lady then?'
'No . . . no . . .' he sighed, and thought of Dorigen.
'What was the reason, tell me, if you can.'
Aurelius in answer then began
To tell the story you have heard before;
There is no need to tell it you once more.
He said 'Arveragus, in his nobleness,
Would rather have died in sorrow and distress
Than that his wife were false to her own word.'
He told him of her grief, that he had heard
She would, that day, have rather lost her life
Than to have proved herself a wicked wife;
'Her vow was made in innocent confusion;
She'd never heard of magical illusion.
And such a sense of pity rose in me
I sent her back as freely then, as he
Had sent her first to me; she went away.
That's the whole story; there's no more to say.'
    And the magician answered, 'My dear brother,

Everich of yow dide gentilly til other.
Thou art a squyer, and he is a knight;
But god forbede, for his blisful might,
But-if a clerk coude doon a gentil dede
As wel as any of yow, it is no drede!

  Sire, I relesse thee thy thousand pound,
As thou right now were cropen out of the ground,
Ne never er now ne haddest knowen me.
For sire, I wol nat take a peny of thee
For al my craft, ne noght for my travaille.
Thou hast y-payed wel for my vitaille;
It is y-nogh, and farewel, have good day:'
And took his hors, and forth he gooth his way.

  Lordinges, this question wolde I aske now,
Which was the moste free, as thinketh yow?
Now telleth me, er that ye ferther wende.
I can na-more, my tale is at an ende.

Each of you did as nobly as the other.
You are a squire, Sir, and he a knight.
But God forbid, in all his blissful might,
That a poor scholar should not come as near
To nobleness as any, never fear.
Sir, I release you of your thousand pound,
No less than if you'd crept out of the ground
Right now, and never had had to do with me.
I will not take a penny, Sir, in fee
For all my knowledge and my work to rid
The coast of rocks; you've paid for what I did,
And paid me well, and that's enough. Good day!
He mounted on his horse and rode away.
My lords, I have a question; answer me!
Which seems to you the noblest of the three?
Now tell me your opinion, everyone,
Ere we go further, for my tale is done.

10. *The Knight's Tale*

lines 1885–1954, with omissions

Swelleth the brest of Arcite, and the sore
Encreesseth at his herte more and more.
The clothered blood, for any lechecraft,
Corrupteth, and is in his bouk y-laft,
That neither veyne-blood, ne ventusinge,
Ne drinke of herbes may ben his helpinge.
The vertu expulsif, or animal,
Fro thilke vertu cleped natural
Ne may the venim voyden, ne expelle.
The pypes of his longes gonne to swelle,
And every lacerte in his brest adoun
Is shent with venim and corrupcioun.
Him gayneth neither, for to gete his lyf,
Vomyt upward, ne dounward laxatif;
Al is to-brosten thilke regioun,
Nature hath now no dominacioun.
And certeinly, ther nature wol nat wirche,
Far-wel, phisyk! go ber the man to chirche!
This al and som, that Arcita mot dye,
For which he sendeth after Emelye,
And Palamon, that was his cosin dere;
Than seyde he thus, as ye shul after here.

'Naught may the woful spirit in myn herte
Declare o poynt of alle my sorwes smerte
To yow, my lady, that I love most;
But I biquethe the service of my gost
To yow aboven every creature,
Sin that my lyf may no lenger dure.
Allas, the wo! allas, the peynes stronge,
That I for yow have suffred, and so longe!
Allas, the deeth! allas, myn Emelye!
Allas, departing of our companye!

THE WORLDS OF HEAVEN, HELL AND DEATH

10. *The Death of Arcite*

Up swells Arcita's breast; the grievous sore
About his heart increases more and more;
The clotting blood, for all the doctor's skill,
Corrupts and festers in his body still,
So neither cupping, bleeding at a vein
Or herbal drink can make him well again;
All, all was shattered and beyond repair,
Nature no longer had dominion there,
And certainly, where Nature cannot work,
Physic, farewell! Go, bear the man to kirk!
This is the sum of all: Arcite must die.

And so he sent for Emily to be by,
And Palamon, the cousin of his heart,
And thus he spoke, preparing to depart:
'Lady, the woeful spirit in my breast,
Of all the griefs by which it is oppressed,
Can nothing speak to you that I love most;
But I bequeathe the service of my ghost
To you above all creatures in the world,
Now that my life is done and banner furled.
Alas the woe, alas the pain, so strong,
That I have suffered for you—and so long!
Alas, O death! Alas, my Emily!
Alas the parting of our company!

Allas, myn hertes quene! allas, my wyf!
Myn hertes lady, endere of my lyf!
What is this world? what asketh men to have?
Now with his love, now in his colde grave
Allone, with-outen any companye.
Far-wel, my swete fo! myn Emelye!
And softe tak me in your armes tweye,
For love of God, and herkneth what I seye.

  I have heer with my cosin Palamon
Had stryf and rancour, many a day a-gon,
For love of yow, and for my jelousye.
And Jupiter so wis my soule gye,
To speken of a servant proprely,
With alle circumstaunces trewely,
That is to seyn, trouthe, honour, and knighthede,
Wisdom, humblesse, estaat, and heigh kinrede,
Fredom, and al that longeth to that art,
So Jupiter have of my soule part,
As in this world right now ne knowe I non
So worthy to ben loved as Palamon,
That serveth yow, and wol don al his lyf.
And if that ever ye shul been a wyf,
Foryet nat Palamon, the gentil man.'
And with that word his speche faille gan,
For from his feet up to his brest was come
The cold of deeth, that hadde him overcome.
And yet more-over, in his armes two
The vital strengthe is lost, and al ago.
Only the intellect, with-outen more,
That dwelled in his herte syk and sore,
Gan faillen, when the herte felte deeth,
Dusked his eyen two, and failled breeth.
But on his lady yet caste he his yë;
His laste word was, 'mercy, Emelye!'
His spirit chaunged hous, and wente ther,
As I cam never, I can nat tellen wher.
Therfor I stinte, I nam no divinistre;
Of soules finde I nat in this registre,

[92]

Alas, Queen of my heart, alas, my wife!
My own heart's lady, ender of my life!
What is this world? What does man ask to have?
Now with his love, now in his cold, cold grave
Alone, alone with none for company!
Farewell my sweetest foe, my Emily!
O softly take me in your arms, I pray,
For the love of God, and hearken what I say.

  I have here, with my cousin Palamon,
Had strife and rancour many a day, now gone,
For love of you, and for my jealousy;
And may Jove's wisdom touch the soul in me
To speak of love and what its service means
Through all the circumstances, all the scenes
Of life—namely good faith and knightly deed,
Honour, humility, and noble breed,
Freedom and truth and openness of heart
And wisdom—as my soul may have its part
With Jove, in all the world I know of none
So worthy to be loved as Palamon,
Who serves you, and will serve you all his life;
And, should you ever choose to be a wife,
Forget not Palamon, that noble man.'
And even as he spoke his speech began
To fail, and from his feet had upward come
The cold of death, and now his breast was numb
And he was vanquished; from his arms there went
The vital power; all was lost and spent;
Only the intellect and nothing more
That dwelt within his heart, so sick and sore,
Began to fail at the approach of death;
Dusked his two eyes at last, and failed his breath,
And still he gazed at her, while he could see,
And his last word was 'Mercy . . . Emily!'
His spirit changed its house and went its way
Where—I was never there and cannot say;
I am no theologian, so, perforce,
Am silent; souls are not mentioned in my source.

11. *Troilus and Criseyde*

Book V, lines 1807–1869

And whan that he was slayn in this manere,
His lighte goost ful blisfully is went
Up to the holownesse of the seventh spere,
In convers letinge every element;
And ther he saugh, with ful avysement,
The erratik sterres, herkeninge armonye
With sownes fulle of hevenish melodye.

And doun from thennes faste he gan avyse
This litel spot of erthe, that with the see
Enbraced is, and fully gan despyse
This wrecched world, and held al vanitee
To respect of the pleyn felicitee
That is in hevene above; and at the laste,
Ther he was slayn, his loking doun he caste;

And in him-self he lough right at the wo
Of hem that wepten for his deeth so faste;
And dampned al our werk that folweth so
The blinde lust, the which that may not laste,
And sholden al our herte on hevene caste.
And forth he wente, shortly for to telle,
Ther as Mercurie sorted him to dwelle.—

---

* Although the general sense of the ascent of Troilus towards 'the full felicity that is in Heaven above' is clear enough, the exact images intended by Chaucer are far from certain. The central earth, with its surrounding elements of water, air and fire, is enclosed in concentric spheres in which move the seven planets (Moon, Mercury, Venus, Sun, Mars, Jupiter, Saturn); in the eighth sphere are found the fixed stars. To an ascending soul looking upwards, each sphere above would seem concave; Chaucer took the idea from a line in Boccaccio's *Teseide: Ver la concavita del cielo ottava.* Chaucer

[94]

11. *The Death of Troilus*

And having fallen to Achilles' spear,
His light soul rose and rapturously went
Towards the concavity of the eighth sphere,
Leaving conversely every element,*
And, as he passed, he saw with wonderment
The wandering planets, hearing harmony,
Whose sound is full of heaven-like melody.

As he looked down there came before his eyes
This little spot of earth, that with the sea
Lies all embraced, and found he could despise
This wretched world, and hold it vanity,
Measured against the full felicity
That is in Heaven above; and, at the last,
To where he had been slain his look he cast.

And inwardly he laughed to see the woes
Of all who mourned his death and wept so fast,
And he condemned all that we do which flows,
From blind desire, that can never last,
When all our thought on Heaven should be cast;
And forth he went, not to be long in telling,
Where Mercury appointed him his dwelling.

---

used the word *holownesse* (hollowness) for *concavita*; in my paraphrase I have reverted to *concavity*, as easier to grasp and nearer modern English. *Conversely* offers further difficulties: Chaucer has '*in convers*' and this may be an error for Boccaccio's *Degli elementi i convessi lasciando*, meaning 'in convex', not 'in converse'; a soul looking downward would see the four elements as in convex spheres below the moon, but in the opposite order, i.e. fire, air, water, earth (*in convers*, or conversely). The planets themselves were sometimes called the 'elements', a fact which adds a further complication.

Swich fyn hath, lo, this Troilus for love,
Swich fyn hath al his grete worthinesse;
Swich fyn hath his estat real above,
Swich fyn his lust, swich fyn hath his noblesse;
Swich fyn hath false worldes brotelnesse.
And thus bigan his lovinge of Criseyde,
As I have told, and in this wyse he deyde.

O yonge fresshe folkes, he or she,
In which that love up groweth with your age,
Repeyreth hoom from worldly vanitee,
And of your herte up-casteth the visage
To thilke god that after his image
Yow made, and thinketh al nis but a fayre
This world, that passeth sone as floures fayre.

And loveth him, the which that right for love
Upon a cros, our soules for to beye,
First starf, and roos, and sit in hevene a-bove;
For he nil falsen no wight, dar I seye,
That wol his herte al hoolly on him leye.
And sin he best to love is, and most meke,
What nedeth feyned loves for to seke?

Lo here, of Payens corsed olde rytes,
Lo here, what alle hir goddes may availle;
Lo here, these wrecched worldes appetytes;
Lo here, the fyn and guerdon for travaille
Of Jove, Apollo, of Mars, of swich rascaille!
Lo here, the forme of olde clerkes speche
In poetrye, if ye hir bokes seche.—

O moral Gower, this book I directe
To thee, and to the philosophical Strode,
To vouchen sauf, ther nede is, to corecte,
Of your benignitees and zeles gode.
And to that sothfast Crist, that starf on rode,
With al myn herte of mercy ever I preye;
And to the lord right thus I speke and seye:

Lo, such an end had Troilus for love,
Lo, such an end his valour, his prowess;
Lo, such an end his royal state above,
Such end his lust, such end his nobleness;
And such an end this false world's brittleness;
And thus began his loving of Criseyde,
As I have told it you, and thus he died.

O all you fresh young people, he or she,
In whom love grows and ripens year by year,
Come home, come home from worldly vanity!
Cast up the countenance of your heart, draw near
To God that made you in His image here,
And think the world is nothing but a fair,
Passing as soon as flower scent in air.

And give your love to Him who, for pure love,
Upon a cross first died that He might pay
Our debt, and rose, and sits in Heaven above;
He will be false to no one that will lay
His heart wholly on Him, I dare to say;
Since He is best to love, and the most meek,
What need is there a feigning love to seek?

Behold these old accursed pagan rites,
Behold how much their gods are worth to you!
Behold these wretched worldly appetites,
Behold your labour's end and guerdon due
From Jove, Apollo and Mars, that rascal crew!
Behold the form in which the ancients speak
Their poetry, if you should care to seek.

O moral Gower, I dedicate this book
To you, and you, my philosophical Strode,
In your benignity and zeal to look,
To warrant, and, where need is, to make good;
And to that truthfast Christ that died on rood,
With all my heart, for mercy ever I pray
And to the Lord right thus I speak and say:

Thou oon, and two, and three, eterne on-lyve,
That regnest ay in three and two and oon,
Uncircumscript, and al mayst circumscryve,
Us from visible and invisible foon
Defende: and to thy mercy, everychoon,
So make us, Jesus, for thy grace, digne,
For love of mayde and moder thyn benigne! Amen.

12. *The Knight's Tale*

lines 2129–2186

'The firste moevere of the cause above,
Whan he first made the faire cheyne of love,
Greet was th'effect, and heigh was his entente;
Wel wiste he why, and what ther-of he mente;
For with that faire cheyne of love he bond
The fyr, the eyr, the water, and the lond
In certeyn boundes, that they may nat flee;
That same prince and that moevere,' quod he,
'Hath stablissed, in this wrecched world adoun,
Certeyne dayes and duracioun
To al that is engendred in this place,
Over the whiche day they may nat pace,
Al mowe they yet tho dayes wel abregge;
Ther needeth non auctoritee allegge,
For it is preved by experience,
But that me list declaren my sentence.
Than may men by this ordre wel discerne,
That thilke moevere stable is and eterne.
Wel may men knowe, but it be a fool,
That every part deryveth from his hool.
For nature hath nat take his beginning
Of no party ne cantel of a thing,
But of a thing that parfit is and stable,
Descending so, til it be corrumpable.

[98]

Thou One and Two and Three and never-ending,
That reignest ever in Three and Two and One,
Incomprehensible, all-comprehending,
From visible foes and the invisible one
Defend us all! And Jesu, Mary's Son,
Make us, in mercy, worthy to be thine,
For love of her, mother and maid benign! Amen.

12. *First Cause and Last Effect*

The First Great Cause and Ruler of all above,
When first He made that fairest chain of love,
Great was the consequence and high the intent;
He well knew why He did, and what He meant;
For, in that fairest chain of love He bound
Fire and Air and Water and the ground
Of Earth in certain bonds they may not flee;
And that same Prince and Mover, even He,
Established this poor world, appointing ways,
Seasons, durations, certain length of days,
To all that is engendered here below,
Past which predestined hour none may go,
Though they have power to abridge their days;
I need not quote authority or raise
More proof than what experience makes clear,
But will put forward my opinion here.
  Well we discern this Order, and are able
To know that Prince as infinite and stable;
Well do we know—all but the fool in soul—
That every part derives from one great whole,
Since Nature cannot be supposed to start
From some particular portion, or mere part,
But from a whole and undisturbed perfection,
Descending thence to what is in subjection

And therfore, of his wyse purveyaunce,
He hath so wel biset his ordinaunce,
That speces of thinges and progressiouns
Shullen enduren by successiouns,
And nat eterne be, with-oute lyë:
This maistow understonde and seen at yë.

'Lo the ook, that hath so long a norisshinge
From tyme that it first biginneth springe,
And hath so long a lyf, as we may see,
Yet at the laste wasted is the tree.

'Considereth eek, how that the harde stoon
Under our feet, on which we trede and goon,
Yit wasteth it, as it lyth by the weye.
The brode river somtyme wexeth dreye.
The grete tounes see we wane and wende.
Than may ye see that al this thing hath ende.

'Of man and womman seen we wel also,
That nedeth, in oon of thise termes two,
This is to seyn, in youthe or elles age,
He moot ben deed, the king as shal a page;
Som in his bed, som in the depe see,
Som in the large feeld, as men may se;
Ther helpeth noght, al goth that ilke weye.
Thanne may I seyn that al this thing moot deye.
What maketh this but Jupiter the king?
The which is prince and cause of alle thing,
Converting al un-to his propre welle,
From which it is deryved, sooth to telle.
And here-agayns no creature on lyve
Of no degree availleth for to stryve.

'Thanne is it wisdom, as it thinketh me,
To maken vertu of necessitee,
And take it wel, that we may nat eschue,
And namely that to us alle is due.

[100]

To chance and change, corruptible; so He,
In wise foreknowledge, stablished His decree
That species of all things, and the progression
Of seed and sex continue by succession,
And not eternally. This is no lie,
As any man can see that has an eye.

  Look at the oak; how slow a tree to nourish
From its first springing till it comes to flourish!
How long a life it has! And yet we see
That in the end it falls, a wasted tree.
Consider too, how hard the stone we tread
Under our feet; that very rock and bed
On which we walk is wasting as it lies.
Time will be when the broadest river dries,
And the great cities wane, and last descend
Into the dust, for all things have an end.

  For men and women we can plainly see
Two terms appointed; so it needs must be;
That is to say the terms of Youth and Age;
For all shall die, the King as shall the Page,
One in his bed, another in deep sea,
Another on the battlefield, may be.
There is no help for it, all take the track,
For all must die, and there is none comes back.
Who orders this but Jupiter the King,
The Prince and Cause of all and everything,
Converting all things back to Him, the Source
From which they were derived, to which they course?
And against this no creature here alive,
Whatever his degree, can hope to strive.
Then it is wisdom, as it seems to me,
To make a virtue of necessity,
And to take well what no one can eschew,
Especially the death that is our due.

13. *The Pardoner's Tale*

lines 333–640

Thise ryotoures three, of whiche I telle,
Longe erst er pryme rong of any belle,
Were set hem in a taverne for to drinke;
And as they satte, they herde a belle clinke
Biforn a cors, was caried to his grave;
That oon of hem gan callen to his knave,
'Go bet,' quod he, 'and axe redily,
What cors is this that passeth heer forby;
And look that thou reporte his name wel.'
'Sir,' quod this boy, 'it nedeth never-a-del.
It was me told, er ye cam heer, two houres;
He was, pardee, an old felawe of youres;
And sodeynly he was y-slayn to-night,
For-dronke, as he sat on his bench upright;
Ther cam a privee theef, men clepeth Deeth,
That in this contree al the peple sleeth,
And with his spere he smoot his herte a-two,
And wente his wey with-outen wordes mo.
He hath a thousand slayn this pestilence:
And, maister, er ye come in his presence,
Me thinketh that it were necessarie
For to be war of swich an adversarie:
Beth redy for to mete him evermore.
Thus taughte me my dame, I sey na-more.'
'By seinte Marie,' seyde this taverner,
'The child seith sooth, for he hath slayn this yeer,
Henne over a myle, with-in a greet village,
Both man and womman, child and hyne, and page.
I trowe his habitacioun be there;
To been avysed greet wisdom it were,

[102]

13. *In Quest of Death*

It's of three rioters I have to tell,
Who, long before the morning service bell,
Were sitting in a tavern for a drink;
And, as they sat, they heard the hand-bell clink
Before a corpse being taken to the grave;
One of them called the little tavern-knave
And said 'Go and find out at once—look spry—
What corpse is in that coffin passing by,
And see you get the name correctly too.'
'Sir,' said the boy, 'no need, I promise you;
Two hours before you came here I was told.
He was a friend of yours in days of old,
And suddenly, last night, Sir, he was slain
Upon his bench, face upwards, drunk again.
There came a privy thief, they call him Death,
Who kills us all round here, and in a breath
He speared him through the heart, he never stirred.
And then Death went away without a word.
He's killed a thousand in the present plague,
And, sir, it doesn't do to be too vague
If you should meet him; you had best be wary.
Be on your guard with such an adversary,
Ready to meet him everywhere you go;
That's what my Mother said; it's all I know.'
'Aye, by St. Mary,' said the publican,
'The child is right, be careful if you can;
This very year he killed, in a large village
A mile away, man, woman, serf at tillage,
Page in the household, children—all there were.
Yes, I imagine that he lives round there;
And I would think it wisdom, I repeat,

Er that he dide a man a dishonour.'
'Ye, goddes armes,' quod this ryotour.
'Is it swich peril with him for to mete?
I shal him seke by wey and eek by strete,
I make avow to goddes digne bones!
Herkneth, felawes, we three been al ones;
Lat ech of us holde up his hond til other,
And ech of us bicomen otheres brother,
And we wol sleen this false traytour Deeth;
He shal be slayn, which that so many sleeth,
By goddes dignitee, er it be night.'

  Togidres han thise three her trouthes plight,
To live and dyen ech of hem for other,
As though he were his owene y-boren brother.
And up they sterte al dronken, in this rage,
And forth they goon towardes that village,
Of which the taverner had spoke biforn,
And many a grisly ooth than han they sworn,
And Cristes blessed body they to-rente—
'Deeth shal be deed, if that they may him hente.'

  Whan they han goon nat fully half a myle,
Right as they wolde han troden over a style,
An old man and a povre with hem mette.
This olde man ful mekely hem grette,
And seyde thus, 'now, lordes, god yow see!'

  The proudest of thise ryotoures three
Answerde agayn, 'what? carl, with sory grace,
Why artow al forwrapped save thy face?
Why livestow so longe in so greet age?'

  This olde man gan loke in his visage,
And seyde thus, 'for I ne can nat finde
A man, though that I walked in-to Inde,
Neither in citee nor in no village,
That wolde chaunge his youthe for myn age;
And therfore moot I han myn age stille,
As longe time as it is goddes wille.

  Ne deeth, allas! ne wol nat han my lyf;

To be prepared for him, in case you meet,
Lest he should do you a dishonour, Sir.'
'What, me? God's arms!' replied this rioter,
'Can meeting with him be so dangerous?
I'll seek him street by street and house by house;
God's blessed bones! I'll register a vow!
Here, chaps; the three of us together now,
Hold up your hands like me, and we'll be brothers
In this affair, and each defend the others,
And we will kill this Death, the treacherous scum,
Who kills so many; now his turn has come,
And, by God's dignity, it shall be to-night!'

   They sealed their bargain, swore with appetite
These three, to live and die for one another,
And to be true as brother is to brother;
Then up they started in their drunken rage
And made towards that village which the page
And publican had spoken of before.
Many and grisly were the oaths they swore,
Tearing Christ's blessed body to a shred:
'If only we can catch him, Death is dead!'

   When they had gone not fully half a mile,
Just as they were about to cross a style,
They met a poor, old man; and at their meeting,
Meekly enough, this old man gave them greeting,
Saying 'May God look kindly on you, Sirs!'
To which the proudest of these rioters
Gave back the answer 'What, old clown? Give place.
Why are you all wrapped up except your face?
Why live so long? Why not get out and die?'

   This ancient fellow looked him in the eye
And said 'Because I never yet have found,
Though I have walked to India searching round
City and village on my pilgrimage,
One who would change his youth to have my age,
And so my age is mine and must be still
Upon me, for such time as God may will.
Not even death, alas, will take my life

Thus walke I, lyk a restelees caityf,
And on the ground, which is my modres gate,
I knokke with my staf, bothe erly and late,
And seye, "leve moder, leet me in!
Lo, how I vanish, flesh, and blood, and skin!
Allas! whan shul my bones been at reste?
Moder, with yow wolde I chaunge my cheste,
That in my chambre longe tyme hath be,
Ye! for an heyre clout to wrappe me!"
But yet to me she wol nat do that grace,
For which ful pale and welked is my face.

  But, sirs, to yow it is no curteisye
To speken to an old man vileinye,
But he trespasse in worde, or elles in dede.
In holy writ ye may your-self wel rede,
"Agayns an old man, hoor upon his heed,
Ye sholde aryse;" wherfor I yeve yow reed,
Ne dooth un-to an old man noon harm now,
Na-more than ye wolde men dide to yow
In age, if that ye so longe abyde;
And god be with yow, wher ye go or ryde.
I moot go thider as I have to go.'

  'Nay, olde cherl, by god, thou shalt nat so,'
Seyde this other hasardour anon;
'Thou partest nat so lightly, by seint John!
Thou spak right now of thilke traitour Deeth,
That in this contree alle our frendes sleeth.
Have heer my trouthe, as thou art his aspye,
Tel wher he is, or thou shalt it abye,
By god, and by the holy sacrament!
For soothly thou art oon of his assent,
To sleen us yonge folk, thou false theef!'

  'Now, sirs,' quod he, 'if that yow be so leef
To finde Deeth, turne up this croked wey,
For in that grove I lafte him, by my fey,
Under a tree, and ther he wol abyde;

So, like a restless prisoner, at strife
Within himself, I walk, I walk and wait;
I walk the ground, which is my mother's gate,
Knock-knocking with my staff from night till noon,
Saying "Dear Mother, open to me soon!
Look at me, Mother! Won't you let me in?
See how I wither, flesh, and blood, and skin!
Alas, when will my bones be laid to rest?
Whatever be the goods within my chest
In my poor room, that has been standing there
So long, I'd barter for a shirt of hair,
Aye, for a shroud! "She has refused her grace,
And therefore pale and withered is my face.

But, Sirs, it showed no courtesy in you
That an old man should have been spoken to
So rudely, though he had done you no offence;
Read Holy Writ, for I derive it thence,
"Thou shalt rise up before the hoary head
And do it honour"; therefore be it said
"Do no more harm to an old man than you,
Being now young, would have another do
To you when old"—if you should live till then.
And so may God be with you, gentlemen,
For I must go whither I have to go.'

'By God, old clown' this gambler shouted 'no!
You don't get off so easy, by St. John!
I heard you mention, just a moment gone,
A certain traitor Death, who singles out
Our friends and kills them, here and round about,
And you're his spy, by God! You wait a bit.
Say where he is or you shall pay for it,
By God and by the Holy Sacrament!
I'll swear you're in it with him by consent,
To kill us younger folk, you thieving swine!'
'Well, Sirs,' he said 'if it be your design
To find where Death is, take this crooked way,
Up to that grove; I left him there, I say,
Under a tree, and there you'll find him waiting.

Nat for your boost he wol him no-thing hyde.
See ye that ook? right ther ye shul him finde.
God save yow, that boghte agayn mankinde,
And yow amende!'—thus seyde this olde man.
And everich of thise ryotoures ran,
Til he cam to that tree, and ther they founde
Of florins fyne of golde y-coyned rounde
Wel ny an eighte busshels, as hem thoughte.
No lenger thanne after Deeth they soughte,
But ech of hem so glad was of that sighte,
For that the florins been so faire and brighte,
That doun they sette hem by this precious hord.
The worste of hem he spake the firste word.

'Brethren,' quod he, 'tak kepe what I seye:
My wit is greet, though that I bourde and pleye.
This tresor hath fortune un-to us yiven,
In mirthe and jolitee our lyf to liven,
And lightly as it comth, so wol we spende.
Ey! goddes precious dignitee! who wende
To-day, that we sholde han so fair a grace?
But mighte this gold be caried fro this place
Hoom to myn hous, or elles un-to youres—
For wel ye woot that al this gold is oures—
Than were we in heigh felicitee.
But trewely, by daye it may nat be;
Men wolde seyn that we were theves stronge,
And for our owene tresor doon us honge.
This tresor moste y-caried be by nighte
As wysly and as slyly as it mighte.
Wherfore I rede that cut among us alle
Be drawe, and lat see wher the cut wol falle;
And he that hath the cut with herte blythe
Shal renne to the toune, and that ful swythe,
And bringe us breed and wyn ful prively.
And two of us shul kepen subtilly
This tresor wel; and, if he wol nat tarie,
Whan it is night, we wol this tresor carie
By oon assent, wher-as us thinketh best.'

[108]

He isn't one to hide, for all your prating.
You see that oak? He won't be far to find.
And God protect you that redeemed mankind,
Aye, and amend you!' Thus said the ancient man.

   At once these three young rioters began
To run, and reached the tree; and there they found
A pile of new gold florins on the ground,
About eight bushels of them, so they thought.
No longer was it Death those fellows sought
For they were all so thrilled to see the sight
—The florins were so beautiful and bright—
That down they sat beside the precious pile;
The wickedest spoke first, after a while.
'Brothers,' he said, 'you listen to what I say;
I'm pretty sharp, although I joke away.
It's clear that Fortune has bestowed this treasure
On us, that we may live in joy and pleasure.
Light come, light go! We'll spend it as we ought.
God's precious dignity! Who would have thought
This morning was to be our lucky day?

   'If only we could get the gold away
Back to my house, or else to yours, perhaps,
—For, as you know, this gold is ours, chaps,
O what a happiness for every one!
But not by day, it simply can't be done.
They'd call us thieves for it, a powerful gang,
And our own property would make us hang.
No, we must bring this treasure back by night
Some prudent way, and keep it out of sight.
And so, as a solution, I propose
We draw for lots, and see the way it goes.
The one who draws the longest, lucky man,
Shall run to town as quickly as he can
To fetch us bread and wine—but keep it dark—
While two remain in hiding here to mark
Our heap of treasure; if there's no delay,
When night comes down, we'll carry it away,
All three of us, wherever we have planned.'

That oon of hem the cut broughte in his fest,
And bad hem drawe, and loke wher it wol falle;
And it fil on the yongeste of hem alle;
And forth toward the toun he wente anon.
And al-so sone as that he was gon,
That oon of hem spak thus un-to that other,
'Thou knowest wel thou art my sworne brother,
Thy profit wol I telle thee anon.
Thou woost wel that our felawe is agon;
And heer is gold, and that ful greet plentee,
That shal departed been among us three.
But natheles, if I can shape it so
That it departed were among us two,
Hadde I nat doon a freendes torn to thee?'

That other answerde, 'I noot how that may be;
He woot how that the gold is with us tweye,
What shal we doon, what shal we to him seye?'

'Shal it be conseil?' seyde the firste shrewe,
'And I shal tellen thee, in wordes fewe,
What we shal doon, and bringe it wel aboute.'

'I graunte,' quod that other, 'out of doute,
That, by my trouthe, I wol thee nat biwreye.'

'Now,' quod the firste, 'thou woost wel we be tweye,
And two of us shul strenger be than oon.
Look whan that he is set, and right anoon
Arys, as though thou woldest with him pleye;
And I shal ryve him thurgh the sydes tweye
Whyl that thou strogelest with him as in game,
And with thy dagger look thou do the same;
And than shal al this gold departed be,
My dere freend, bitwixen me and thee;
Than may we bothe our lustes al fulfille,
And pleye at dees right at our owene wille.'
And thus acorded been thise shrewes tweye
To sleen the thridde, as ye han herd me seye.

This yongest, which that wente un-to the toun,
Ful ofte in herte he rolleth up and doun
The beautee of thise florins newe and brighte.

He gathered lots and hid them in his hand,
Bidding them draw for where the luck would fall.
It fell upon the youngest of them all,
And off he ran at once, towards the town.
As soon as he had gone, the first sat down
And thus began to parley with the other:
'You know that you can trust me like a brother;
I mean to tell you where your profit lies.
You know our friend has gone to fetch supplies,
And here's a lot of gold that is to be
Divided equally, between us three.
Nevertheless, if I could shape it thus,
So that we shared it out—the two of us—
Wouldn't you take it as a friendly turn?'
'But how?' the other said with some concern,
'He knows the gold is here with me and you;
What can we tell him? What are we to do?'
'Is it a bargain,' said the first, 'or no?
For I can tell you in a word or so
What's to be done to bring the thing about.'
'Trust me,' the other said, 'you needn't doubt
My word of honour; I will play you fair.'
'Well,' said his friend, 'here's two of us, a pair;
And two are twice as powerful as one.
Now look; when he comes back, get up in fun
As if to wrestle with him; you attack,
And I will put a dagger through his back
While you and he are struggling, as in game;
And see you draw your knife and do the same.
Then all the money will be ours to spend,
Divided equally of course, dear friend,
Then we can gratify our lusts and fill
Our days with dicing, at our own sweet will.'
So these two miscreants agreed to slay
The third and youngest, as you heard me say.

This youngest, as he ran towards the town,
Kept turning over, rolling up and down
Within his heart the beauty of those bright

'O lord!' quod he, 'if so were that I mighte
Have al this tresor to my-self allone,
Ther is no man that liveth under the trone
Of god, that sholde live so mery as I!'
And atte laste the feend, our enemy,
Putte in his thought that he shold poyson beye,
With which he mighte sleen his felawes tweye;
For-why the feend fond him in swich lyvinge,
That he had leve him to sorwe bringe,
For this was outrely his fulle entente
To sleen hem bothe, and never to repente.
And forth he gooth, no lenger wolde he tarie,
Into the toun, un-to a pothecarie,
And preyed him, that he him wolde selle
Som poyson, that he mighte his rattes quelle;
And eek ther was a polcat in his hawe,
That, as he seyde, his capouns hadde y-slawe,
And fayn he wolde wreke him, if he mighte,
On vermin, that destroyed him by nighte.

    The pothecarie answerde, 'and thou shalt have
A thing that, al-so god my soule save,
In al this world ther nis no creature,
That ete or dronke hath of this confiture
Noght but the mountance of a corn of whete,
That he ne shal his lyf anon forlete;
Ye, sterve he shal, and that in lasse whyle
Than thou wolt goon a paas nat but a myle;
This poyson is so strong and violent.'

    This cursed man hath in his hond y-hent
This poyson in a box, and sith he ran
In-to the nexte strete, un-to a man,
And borwed [of] him large botels three;
And in the two his poyson poured he;
The thridde he kepte clene for his drinke.
For al the night he shoop him for to swinke
In caryinge of the gold out of that place.

New florins, saying 'Lord, if I only might
Have all this treasure to myself alone,
Could there be anyone beneath the throne
Of God so happy as I then should be?'
At last the Fiend, our common enemy,
Using his power to put it in his thought
That there was always poison to be bought,
Pointed a way in which to kill his friends.
To men in such a state the Devil sends
Thoughts of this kind, and has a full permission
To lure them on to sorrow and perdition;
For this young man was utterly content
To slay them both, and never to repent.

So on he ran, he had no thought to tarry,
Came to the town, found an apothecary,
And said 'Sell me some poison, if you will,
There are some rats of mine I want to kill,
And there's a polecat too about my yard,
That takes my chickens and it hits me hard,
But I'll get even, as is only right,
With vermin that destroy a man by night.'

The chemist answered 'I've a preparation
Which you shall have, and by my soul's salvation,
If any living creature eat or drink
Of it, before he has the time to think,
Though he took less than makes a grain of wheat,
He will at once fall dying at your feet;
Yes, die he must, and in so short a while,
You'd hardly have the time to walk a mile,
This poison is so strong, you understand.'

This cursed fellow grabbed into his hand
This poison in a box, and off he ran
Into a neighbouring street, and found a man
Who lent him three large bottles; he withdrew
And quickly poured his poison into two;
The third one he kept clean, for his own drinking;
For he would need it later, he was thinking,
Stacking the gold and getting it away.

And whan this ryotour, with sory grace,
Had filled with wyn his grete botels three,
To his felawes agayn repaireth he.
　What nedeth it to sermone of it more?
For right as they had cast his deeth bifore,
Right so they han him slayn, and that anon.
And whan that this was doon, thus spak that oon,
'Now lat us sitte and drinke, and make us merie,
And afterward we wol his body berie.'
And with that word it happed him, par cas,
To take the botel ther the poyson was,
And drank, and yaf his felawe drinke also,
For which anon they storven bothe two.
　But, certes, I suppose that Avicen
Wroot never in no canon, ne in no fen,
Mo wonder signes of empoisoning
Than hadde thise wrecches two, er hir ending.
Thus ended been thise homicydes two,
And eek the false empoysoner also.

14. *The Friar's Tale*

lines 77–346, with omissions

　And so bifel, that ones on a day
This Somnour, ever waiting on his pray,
Rood for to somne a widwe, an old ribybe,
Feyninge a cause, for he wolde brybe.
And happed that he saugh bifore him ryde
A gay yeman, under a forest-syde.
A bowe he bar, and arwes brighte and kene;
He hadde up-on a courtepy of grene;
An hat up-on his heed with frenges blake.
　'Sir,' quod this Somnour, 'hayl! and wel a-take!'
'Wel-come,' quod he, 'and every good felawe!
Wher rydestow under this grene shawe?'

And when this rioter, this devil's clay,
Had filled his bottles up with wine, all three,
Back to rejoin his comrades sauntered he.
What need to sermonise? A waste of breath!
Exactly in the way they'd planned his death,
They fell on him and slew him, two to one;
Then said the first of them, when this was done,
'Now for a drink; sit down, and let's be merry,
For later on there'll be the corpse to bury.'
And, as it happened, reaching for a sup,
He took a bottle full of poison up
And drank; and his companion, nothing loath,
Drank from it also, and they perished both.

There is, in Avicenna's long narration
Concerning poison in its operation,
No paragraph more horrible, transcending
What these two wretches suffered at their ending.
Thus these two murderers received their due;
So did the treacherous young poisoner too.

14. *How Devils Make a Living*

So it befell upon a certain day
This Summoner rode forth to take his prey,
A poor old fiddle of the widow-tribe,
From whom, on a feigned charge, he hoped a bribe.
Now, as he rode, it happened that he saw
A gay young yeoman under a leafy shaw;
He bore a bow with arrows bright and keen
And wore a little jacket of bright green
And had a black-fringed hat upon his head.
'Hail! Welcome and well met!' the Summoner said.
'Welcome to you, and all good lads!' said he;
'Whither away under the greenwood tree?'

Seyde this yeman, 'wiltow fer to day?'

This Somnour him answerde, and seyde, 'nay;
Heer faste by,' quod he, 'is myn entente
To ryden, for to reysen up a rente
That longeth to my lordes duëtee.'

'Artow thanne a bailly?' 'Ye!' quod he.
He dorste nat, for verray filthe and shame,
Seye that he was a somnour, for the name.

'*Depardieux*,' quod this yeman, 'dere brother,
Thou art a bailly, and I am another.
I am unknowen as in this contree;
Of thyn aqueyntance I wolde praye thee,
And eek of brotherhede, if that yow leste.
I have gold and silver in my cheste;
If that thee happe to comen in our shyre,
Al shal be thyn, right as thou wolt desyre.'

'Grantmercy,' quod this Somnour, 'by my feith!'
Everich in otheres hand his trouthe leith,
For to be sworne bretheren til they deye.
In daliance they ryden forth hir weye.

This Somnour, which that was as ful of jangles,
As ful of venim been thise wariangles,
And ever enquering up-on every thing,
'Brother,' quod he, 'where is now your dwelling,
Another day if that I sholde yow seche?'

This yeman him answerde in softe speche,
'Brother,' quod he, 'fer in the north contree,
Wher, as I hope, som-tyme I shal thee see.
Er we departe, I shal thee so wel wisse,
That of myn hous ne shaltow never misse.'

'Now, brother,' quod this Somnour, 'I yow preye,
Teche me, whyl that we ryden by the weye,
Sin that ye been a baillif as am I,
Som subtiltee, and tel me feithfully
In myn offyce how I may most winne;
And spareth nat for conscience ne sinne,
But as my brother tel me, how do ye?'

'Now, by my trouthe, brother dere,' seyde he,

[116]

Pursued the yeoman, 'have you far to go?'
The Summoner paused a moment and said 'No,
Just here, close by. In fact I'm only bent
On going for a ride to raise a rent
That's owing to my lord—a little fee.'
'Why then, you are a bailiff?' 'Yes', said he;
(He didn't dare, for very filth and shame,
Say that he was a summoner—for the name).
'Well, I'll be damned!' the yeoman said, 'dear brother,
You say you are a bailiff? I'm another.
But I'm unknown—a stranger in the land;
I'll beg acquaintance of you, and the hand
Of brotherhood, if that is fair to offer;
I have some gold and silver in my coffer,
And, should you chance to come into our shire,
All shall be yours, as much as you desire.'
'My word!' the Summoner answered 'thanks a lot!'
The pair of them shook hands upon the spot,
Swore to be brothers till their dying day,
And, chatting pleasantly, rode on their way.

  This Summoner, always ready with a word
As full of venom as a butcher-bird,
Sticking his nose in one thing or another,
Went on 'And where do you live at home, dear brother?
I might come calling there some other day.'
The yeoman said in his soft-spoken way
'O, far away up north; I'll tell you where,
And I shall hope, some time, to see you there;
Before we part I shall be so explicit
As to my house, I'm sure you'll never miss it.'
'Brother,' the Summoner said, 'I'd like to know
If you would teach me something as we go.
Since you're a bailiff just the same as me,
Teach me, I beg of you, some subtlety
For making the best money at our game?
Keep nothing back for conscience, or from shame,
Talk like a brother; how do you make out?'
'Well, I break level, brother, just about,

'As I shal tellen thee a feithful tale,
My wages been ful streite and ful smale.
My lord is hard to me and daungerous,
And myn offyce is ful laborous;
And therfore by extorcions I live.
For sothe, I take al that men wol me yive;
Algate, by sleyghte or by violence,
Fro yeer to yeer I winne al my dispence.
I can no bettre telle feithfully.'

'Now, certes,' quod this Somnour, 'so fare I;
I spare nat to taken, god it woot,
But-if it be to hevy or to hoot.
What I may gete in conseil prively,
No maner conscience of that have I;
Nere myn extorcioun, I mighte nat liven,
Ne of swiche japes wol I nat be shriven.
Stomak ne conscience ne knowe I noon;
I shrewe thise shrifte-fadres everichoon.
Wel be we met, by god and by seint Jame!
But, leve brother, tel me than thy name,'
Quod this Somnour; and in this mene whyle,
This yeman gan a litel for to smyle.

'Brother,' quod he, 'wiltow that I thee telle?
I am a feend, my dwelling is in helle.
And here I ryde about my purchasing,
To wite wher men wolde yeve me any thing.
My purchas is th'effect of al my rente.
Loke how thou rydest for the same entente,
To winne good, thou rekkest never how;
Right so fare I, for ryde wolde I now
Un-to the worldes ende for a preye.'

'A,' quod this Somnour, *'ben'cite*, what sey ye?
I wende ye were a yeman trewely.
Ye han a mannes shap as wel as I;
Han ye figure than determinat
In helle, ther ye been in your estat?'

'Nay, certeinly,' quod he, 'ther have we noon;
But whan us lyketh, we can take us oon,

[118]

I'll tell a truthful story; all in all,
My wages are extremely tight and small.
My master's hard on me and difficult,
My job laborious and with poor result,
And so its by extortion that I live;
I take whatever anyone will *give*;
At any rate, by tricks and violences,
From year to year I cover my expenses,
I can't say better, speaking truthfully.'
The Summoner said 'It's just the same with me;
I'm ready to take anything, God wot,
Unless it be too heavy, or too hot.
What I can get out of a little chat
In private—why should conscience boggle at that?
Without extortion, how could I make a living?
My little jokes are hardly worth forgiving.
Bowels of pity, conscience, I have none;
Plague on these penance-fathers, every one!
We are well met, by God and by St. James!
But, brother, what do you say to swopping names?'
This Summoner paused; the yeoman all the while
He had been speaking, wore a little smile;
'Brother,' he answered, 'would you have me tell?
I am a fiend; my dwelling is in Hell.
I ride on business and have so far thriven
By taking everything that I am given;
That is the gross of all my revenue.
You seem to have the same objective too,
You're out for wealth, acquired no matter how,
And so with me; I'll go a-riding now
As far as the world's end in search of prey.'
'Lord!' said the Summoner, 'what did I hear you say?
I thought you were a yeoman, honestly;
You have the body of a man, like me;
And have you then another shape as well
Appointed for your high estate in Hell?'
'No,' he replied, 'for Hell admits of none;
But when we like we can appropriate one,

Or elles make yow seme we ben shape
Som-tyme lyk a man, or lyk an ape;
Or lyk an angel can I ryde or go.
It is no wonder thing thogh it be so;
A lousy jogelour can deceyve thee,
And pardee, yet can I more craft than he.'

'Why,' quod the Somnour, 'ryde ye thanne or goon
In sondry shap, and nat alwey in oon?'

'For we,' quod he, 'wol us swich formes make
As most able is our preyes for to take.'

'What maketh yow to han al this labour?'

'Ful many a cause, leve sir Somnour,'
Seyde this feend, 'but alle thing hath tyme.
The day is short, and it is passed pryme,
And yet ne wan I no-thing in this day.
I wol entende to winnen, if I may,
And nat entende our wittes to declare.
For, brother myn, thy wit is al to bare
To understonde, al-thogh I tolde hem thee.
But, for thou axest why labouren we;
For, som-tyme, we ben goddes instruments,
And menes to don his comandements,
Whan that him list, up-on his creatures,
In divers art and in divers figures.
With-outen him we have no might, certayn,
If that him list to stonden ther-agayn.
And som-tyme, at our prayere, han we leve
Only the body and nat the soule greve;
Witnesse on Job, whom that we diden wo.
And som-tyme han we might of bothe two,
This is to seyn, of soule and body eke.
And somtyme be we suffred for to seke
Up-on a man, and doon his soule unreste,
And nat his body, and al is for the beste.
Whan he withstandeth our temptacioun,
It is a cause of his savacioun;
Al-be-it that it was nat our entente
He sholde be sauf, but that we wolde him hente.

[120]

Or rather make you think we have a shape,
It could be like a man, or like an ape,
Or like an angel riding into bliss;
There's nothing very wonderful in this;
A lousy conjuror can trick your eye,
Yet he, God knows, has far less power than I.'
'But why' pursued the Summoner, 'track your game
In various shapes? Why don't you stay the same?'
'Just to appear' he said 'in such a way
As will enable us to catch our prey.'
'But why take so much trouble—all this stir?'
'For many a reason, good Sir Summoner;
You shall know all about it in good time.
The day is short and it is long past prime,
And yet I've taken nothing the whole day;
I have to think of business, if I may,
Rather than air my intellectual gift;
Besides, you lack the brains to catch my drift.
If I explained you wouldn't understand;
Yet, since you ask why we're a busy band,
It's thus: at times we are God's instruments,
A means of forwarding divine events,
When He so pleases, that concern His creatures
By various arts, disguised in various features.
We have no power without Him, that's a fact,
If it should please Him to oppose some act.
Sometimes, at our request, He gives us leave
To hurt the body, though we may not grieve
The soul; take Job. His is a case in point.
At other times the two are not disjoint,
That is to say, the body and the soul.
Sometimes we are allowed to take control
Over a man and put his soul to test,
But not his body; and all is for the best,
For, every time a man withstands temptation,
It is a partial cause of his salvation,
Though our intention is, when we beset him,
Not that he should be saved, but we should get him.

And som-tyme be we servant un-to man,
As to the erchebisshop Seint Dunstan
And to the apostles servant eek was I.'

'Yet tel me,' quod the Somnour, 'feithfully,
Make ye yow newe bodies thus alway
Of elements?' the feend answerde, 'nay;
Som-tyme we feyne, and som-tyme we aryse
With dede bodies in ful sondry wyse,
And speke as renably and faire and wel
As to the Phitonissa dide Samuel.
And yet wol som men seye it was nat he;
I do no fors of your divinitee.
But o thing warne I thee, I wol nat jape,
Thou wolt algates wite how we ben shape;
Thou shalt her-afterward, my brother dere,
Com ther thee nedeth nat of me to lere.
For thou shalt by thyn owene experience
Conne in a chayer rede of this sentence
Bet than Virgyle, whyl he was on lyve,
Or Dant also; now lat us ryde blyve.
And right at the entring of the tounes ende,
To which this Somnour shoop him for to wende,
They saugh a cart, that charged was with hey,
Which that a carter droof forth in his wey.
Deep was the wey, for which the carte stood.
The carter smoot, and cryde, as he were wood,
'Hayt, Brok! hayt, Scot! what spare ye for the stones?
The feend,' quod he, 'yow fecche body and bones,
As ferforthly as ever were ye foled!
So muche wo as I have with yow tholed!
The devel have al, bothe hors and cart and hey!'

This Somnour seyde, 'heer shal we have a pley;'
And neer the feend he drough, as noght ne were,
Ful prively, and rouned in his ere:
'Herkne, my brother, herkne, by thy feith;
Herestow nat how that the carter seith?
Hent it anon, for he hath yeve it thee,
Bothe hey and cart, and eek hise caples three.'

At times we slave for men without complaint,
As for Archbishop Dunstan, now a Saint;
Why, I was servant to the Apostle Paul.'
'Do tell me,' said the Summoner, 'tell me all;
Do you create new bodies, as you go,
Out of the elements?' The Fiend said 'No;
We just create illusions, or we raise
A corpse, and use it; there are many ways,
And we can talk as trippingly and well
As to the Witch of Endor, Samuel.
And yet some men will say it wasn't he;
I have no use for your theology.
One thing I warn you of, it is no jape;
You soon will know for sure about our shape;
Hereafterward, dear brother, you shall be
Where you shall have no need to learn of me.
But from your own experience declare,
As much as from a professorial chair,
Better than even Virgil hereupon,
Or Dante either; now let's hurry on' . . .

  Just at the entry of the very village
The Summoner had it in his mind to pillage,
They saw a farm-cart, loaded up with hay;
There was a carter driving, but the way
Was deep and muddy and the cart stood still.
The carter lashed and shouted with a will
'Hey, Brock! Hup, Scottie! Never mind for stones!
The foul Fiend fetch you all, body and bones,
As sure as you were foaled! Mud, ruts and rubble!
Lord, what a team! I've never known such trouble.
The Devil take all, cart, horses and hay in one!'
The Summoner said 'Now we shall have some fun!'
And, as if nothing were happening, he drew near
And whispered softly in the Devil's ear
'Listen to that, dear brother, use your head!
Didn't you hear what that old carter said?
Take them at once, he gave them all to you,
His hay, his cart and his three horses too.'

[123]

'Nay,' quod the devel, 'god wot, never a deel;
It is nat his entente, trust me weel.
Axe him thy-self, if thou nat trowest me,
Or elles stint a while, and thou shalt see.'

This carter thakketh his hors upon the croupe,
And they bigonne drawen and to-stoupe;
'Heyt, now!' quod he, 'ther Jesu Crist yow blesse,
And al his handwerk, bothe more and lesse!
That was wel twight, myn owene lyard boy!
I pray god save thee and sëynt Loy!
Now is my cart out of the slow, pardee!'

'Lo! brother,' quod the feend, 'what tolde I thee?
Heer may ye see, myn owene dere brother,
The carl spak oo thing, but he thoghte another.
Lat us go forth abouten our viage;
Heer winne I no-thing up-on cariage.'

Whan that they comen som-what out of toune,
This Somnour to his brother gan to roune,
'Brother,' quod he, 'heer woneth an old rebekke,
That hadde almost as lief to lese hir nekke
As for to yeve a peny of hir good.
I wol han twelf pens, though that she be wood,
Or I wol sompne hir un-to our offyce;
And yet, god woot, of hir knowe I no vyce.
But for thou canst nat, as in this contree,
Winne thy cost, tak heer ensample of me.'

This Somnour clappeth at the widwes gate.
'Com out,' quod he, 'thou olde viritrate!
I trowe thou hast som frere or preest with thee!'

'Who clappeth?' seyde this widwe, '*ben'cite!*
God save you, sire, what is your swete wille?'

'I have,' quod he, 'of somonce here a bille;
Up peyne of cursing, loke that thou be
To-morn bifore the erchedeknes knee
T'answere to the court of certeyn thinges.'

'Now, lord,' quod she, 'Crist Jesu, king of kinges,
So wisly helpe me, as I ne may.
I have been syk, and that ful many a day.

[124]

'Don't you believe it!' said the Fiend; 'I heard,
But he meant nothing by it, take my word;
Go up and ask him, if you don't trust me,
Or else keep quiet for a bit and see.'
The carter thwacked his horses, jerked the rein
And got them moving; as they took the strain
'Hup there!' he shouted, 'Jesus bless you, love,
And all His handiwork! Hey, Saints above!
Well tugged, old fellow, that's the stuff, Grey Boy!
God save you all, my darlings! Send you joy!
That's lifted the old cart out of the slough!'
'What did I tell you' said the Fiend 'just now?
That ought to make it clear to you, dear brother,
The chap said one thing, but he thought another.
So let's go on a bit; you mustn't scoff,
But here there's nothing I can carry off.'
A little out of town, the Summoner leaned
Across, and started whispering to the Fiend:
'There's an old fiddle here, an ancient wreck,
Dear brother, who would rather break her neck
Than lose a penny of her goods. Too bad,
She'll have to pay me twelve pence; she'll be mad,
But if she doesn't pay, she'll face the court.
And yet, God knows, there's nothing to report,
She has no vices; but, as you failed just now,
To earn your keep here, I will show you how.'

The Summoner battered at the widow's gate.
'Come out,' he said 'you old inebriate!
I'll bet you've got a friar or priest inside!'
'Who's knocking! Bless us, Lord!' the widow cried,
'God save you, Sir; and what is your sweet will?'
'I have' the Summoner said 'a summons-bill;
On pain of excommunication, see
That you're at court, at the Archdeacon's knee,
Tomorrow morning; there are certain things
To answer for.' 'Christ Jesus, King of Kings,
Help me!' she said 'I neither can nor may,
I have been sick, aye, and for many a day;

I may nat go so fer,' quod she, 'ne ryde,
But I be deed, so priketh it in my syde.
May I nat axe a libel, sir Somnour,
And answere there, by my procutour,
To swich thing as men wol opposen me?'

'Yis,' quod this Somnour, 'pay anon, lat se,
Twelf pens to me, and I wol thee acquyte.
I shall no profit han ther-by but lyte;
My maister hath the profit, and nat I.
Com of, and lat me ryden hastily;
Yif me twelf pens, I may no lenger tarie.'

'Twelf pens,' quod she, 'now lady Seinte Marie
So wisly help me out of care and sinne,
This wyde world thogh that I sholde winne,
Ne have I nat twelf pens with-inne myn hold.
Ye knowen wel that I am povre and old;
Kythe your almesse on me povre wrecche.'

'Nay than,' quod he, 'the foule feend me fecche
If I th'excuse, though thou shul be spilt!'

'Alas,' quod she, god woot, I have no gilt.'

'Pay me,' quod he, 'or by the swete seinte Anne,
As I wol bere awey thy newe panne
For dette, which that thou owest me of old,
Whan that thou madest thyn housbond cokewold,
I payde at hoom for thy correccioun.'

'Thou lixt,' quod she, 'by my savacioun!
Ne was I never er now, widwe ne wyf,
Somoned un-to your court in al my lyf;
Ne never I nas but of my body trewe!
Un-to the devel blak and rough of hewe
Yeve I thy body and my panne also!'

And whan the devel herde hir cursen so
Up-on hir knees, he seyde in this manere,
'Now Mabely, myn owene moder dere,
Is this your wil in ernest, that ye seye?'

'The devel,' quod she, 'so fecche him er he deye,
And panne and al, but he wol him repente!'

'Nay, olde stot, that is nat myn entente,'

[126]

I couldn't walk so far' she said, 'or ride,
'Twould kill me; there's a pricking in my side.
Couldn't you write it down, to save the journey,
And I could answer it through my attorney,
The charge, I mean; whatever it may be?'

   'Yes, if you pay at once,' he said, 'let's see;
Twelve pence to me, and I'll secure acquittal;
I get no profit from it—very little;
My master gets the profit and not me;
Come off it, I'm in haste; it's got to be.
Give me twelve pence; no time to wait, old fairy.'

   'Twelve pence!' she cried, 'O blessed Virgin Mary,
Help me and keep me clear of sin and dearth!
Why, if you were to offer me the earth,
I couldn't! There's not twelve pence in my bag!
You know I'm nothing but a poor old hag;
Show kindness to a miserable wretch!'
If I excuse you, may the Devil fetch
Me off, though it should break you! Come along,
Pay up!' 'Alas, but I've done nothing wrong.'
'Pay me at once, or, by the sweet St. Anne,'
He said 'I'll carry off your frying-pan
For debt, the new one, owed me since the day
You cuckolded your husband. Did I pay
For your correction, then, or did I not?'
'You lie!' she said 'by my salvation! What?
Correction! Whether as widow or as wife,
I've never had a summons in my life;
I never cuckolded my poor old man!
And as for you and for my frying-pan,
The hairiest, blackest devil out of Hell,
I give you to him! And the pan as well!'

   Seeing her kneel and curse, the Devil spoke:
'Now, Mother Mabel, is this all a joke,
Or do you really mean the things you say?'
'The Devil' she said 'can carry him away
With pan and all—unless he will repent.'
'No, you old cow, I have no such intent,'

Quod this Somnour, 'for to repente me,
For any thing that I have had of thee;
I wolde I hadde thy smok and every clooth!'
   'Now, brother,' quod the devel, 'be nat wrooth;
Thy body and this panne ben myne by right.
Thou shalt with me to helle yet to-night,
Where thou shalt knowen of our privetee
More than a maister of divinitee:'
And with that word this foule feend him hente;
Body and soule, he with the devel wente
Wher-as that somnours han hir heritage.
And god, that maked after his image
Mankinde, save and gyde us alle and some;
And leve this Somnour good man to bicome!

15. *The Prologue to the Summoner's Tale*

lines 1–42

This Somnour in his stiropes hye stood;
Up-on this Frere his herte was so wood,
That lyk an aspen leef he quook for yre.
   'Lordinges,' quod he, 'but o thing I desyre;
I yow biseke that, of your curteisye,
Sin ye han herd this false Frere lye,
As suffereth me I may my tale telle!
This Frere bosteth that he knoweth helle,
And god it woot, that it is litel wonder;
Freres and feendes been but lyte a-sonder.
For pardee, ye han ofte tyme herd telle,
How that a frere ravisshed was to helle
In spirit ones by a visioun;
And as an angel ladde him up and doun,
To shewen him the peynes that ther were,
In al the place saugh he nat a frere;
Of other folk he saugh y-nowe in wo.

The Summoner said, 'there's no repentance due
For anything I ever had of you;
I'll strip you naked, smock and rag and clout!'
   The Devil said 'What are you cross about,
Dear brother? You and this pan are mine by right,
You yet shall be in Hell with me to-night,
Where you'll learn more about our mystery
Than any Doctor of Divinity.'
   And on the word, this foul Fiend made a swoop
And bore him, body and soul, to join the troupe
In Hell, where Summoners have their special shelf.
And God, who, in the image of Himself
Created man, guide us to Abraham's lap,
And make this Summoner here a decent chap!

15. *How a Friar Visited Hell*

The Summoner rose in wrath against the Friar
High in his stirrups, and he quaked with ire;
He stood there trembling like an aspen leaf.
'I've only one desire,' he said, 'it's brief,
And one your courtesy will not deny.
Since you have heard this filthy Friar lie,
I beg you listen to my tale as well.
This Friar boasts his knowledge about Hell,
And God He knows that that's but little wonder;
Friars and Fiends are seldom far asunder.
Heavens, you must have often heard them tell
Of how a Friar was ravished down to Hell
Once in a vision, taken there in spirit.
An angel led him up and down to ferret
Among the torments of eternal fire
And yet he did not see a single friar,
Though he saw many other kinds of folk

Un-to this angel spak the frere tho:
  "Now, sir," quod he, "han freres swich a grace
That noon of hem shal come to this place?"
  "Yis," quod this angel, "many a millioun!"
And un-to Sathanas he ladde him doun.
"And now hath Sathanas," seith he, "a tayl
Brodder than of a carrik is the sayl.
Hold up thy tayl, thou Sathanas!" quod he,
"Shewe forth thyn ers, and lat the frere see
Wher is the nest of freres in this place!"
And, er that half a furlong-wey of space,
Right so as bees out swarmen from an hyve,
Out of the develes ers ther gonne dryve
Twenty thousand freres in a route,
And thurgh-out helle swarmeden aboute
And comen agayn, as faste as they may gon,
And in his ers they crepten everichon.
He clapte his tayl agayn, and lay ful stille.
This frere, whan he loked hadde his fille
Upon the torments of this sory place,
His spirit god restored of his grace
Un-to his body agayn, and he awook;
But natheles, for fere yet he quook,
So was the develes ers ay in his minde,
That is his heritage of verray kinde.

[130]

In pain enough. At last this friar spoke:
"Sir, are the friars in such a state of grace"
He said "none ever come into this place?"
"Why, yes," the angel answered, "many a million!"
And led him down to Satan's high pavillion.
"Satan" the angel said "has got a tail
As broad or broader than a galleon sail.
Hold up thy tail, thou Satan!" then said he
"Show forth thine arse, and let this friar see
The nest ordained for friars in this place!"
   Ere the tail rose a furlong into space,
From underneath it there began to drive
(Much as if bees were swarming from a hive)
Some twenty thousand friars in a rout,
Who swarmed all over Hell and round about
And then came back, as fast as they could run,
And crept into his arse again, each one.
He clapped his tail on them and then lay still.
And after, when the friar had looked his fill
On all the torments in that sorry place
His spirit was restored, by Heaven's grace,
Back to his body again and he awoke;
Nevertheless the terror made him choke,
So much the Devil's arse was in his mind,
The natural heritage of all his kind.

16. *The Parliament of Fowls*

lines 99–105

The wery hunter, slepinge in his bed,
To wode ayein his minde goth anoon;
The juge dremeth how his plees ben sped;
The carter dremeth how his cartes goon;
The riche, of gold; the knight fight with his foon,
The seke met he drinketh of the tonne;
The lover met he hath his lady wonne.

17. *Troilus and Criseyde*

Book II, lines 918–931

A nightingale, upon a cedre grene,
Under the chambre-wal ther as she lay,
Ful loude sang ayein the mone shene,
Paraunter, in his briddes wyse, a lay
Of love, that made hir herte fresh and gay
That herkned she so longe in good entente.
Til at the laste the dede sleep hir hente.

And, as she sleep, anoon-right tho hir mette,
How that an egle, fethered whyt as boon,
Under hir brest his longe clawes sette,
And out hir herte he rente, and that a-noon,
And dide his herte in-to hir brest to goon,
Of which she nought agroos ne no-thing smerte,
And forth he fleigh, with herte left for herte.

THE WORLD OF DREAMS

16. *One Theory of the Nature of Dreams*

The weary hunter, sleeping in his bed,
In mind goes out into the woods again;
The Judge will dream of how his pleas have sped,
The carter how his carts will take the strain;
The rich of gold: the Knight of might and main;
The sick of healthy drinking from the tun;
The lover dreams his lady has been won.

17. *A Lady Dreams of her Lover*

A nightingale upon a cedar green,
Under the chamber window where she lay,
Sang loudly out against the moony sheen
And it may well have sung, in its bird's way,
A song of love; her heart grew light and gay,
And long she lay and listened, then could keep
Awake no longer, and fell dead asleep.

At once a dream ascended on her rest;
There came an eagle, feathered white as bone,
Who set his curving talons to her breast
And tore her heart out, giving her his own
Into her body, left her there alone
—And yet she suffered neither fear nor smart—
And flew away, leaving her heart for heart.

18. *Troilus and Criseyde*

Book V, lines 1233–1288

So on a day he leyde him doun to slepe,
And so bifel that in his sleep him thoughte,
That in a forest faste he welk to wepe
For love of hir that him these peynes wroughte;
And up and doun as he the forest soughte,
He mette he saugh a boor with tuskes grete,
That sleep ayein the brighte sonnes hete.

And by this boor, faste in his armes folde,
Lay kissing ay his lady bright Criseyde:
For sorwe of which, whan he it gan biholde,
And for despyt, out of his slepe he breyde,
And loude he cryde on Pandarus, and seyde,
'O Pandarus, now knowe I crop and rote!
I nam but deed, ther nis non other bote!

My lady bright Criseyde hath me bitrayed,
In whom I trusted most of any wight,
She elles-where hath now hir herte apayed;
The blisful goddes, through hir grete might,
Han in my dreem y-shewed it ful right.
Thus in my dreem Criseyde I have biholde'—
And al this thing to Pandarus he tolde.

'O my Criseyde, allas! what subtiltee,
What newe lust, what beautee, what science,
What wratthe of juste cause have ye to me?
What gilt of me, what fel experience
Hath fro me raft, allas! thyn advertence?
O trust, O feyth, O depe aseuraunce,
Who hath me reft Criseyde, al my plesaunce?

[134]

18. *A Lover Dreams of his Lady*

And then, one evening, he lay down to sleep;
He had a dream; it seemed to him in thought
That he had walked into the woods to weep
For her, and for the grief that she had brought;
And, up and down the forest, as he sought
His way, he came upon a tusky boar,
Asleep upon the sunny forest floor.

And close beside it, with her arms enfolding
And ever kissing it, he saw Criseyde;
The grief he suffered as he stood beholding
Burst all the bonds of sleep, and, at a stride,
He was awake and in despair, and cried
'O Pandar, now I see it through and through!
I am but dead, there is no more to do.

'My own bright lady has not played me fair;
She that I trusted most is now proved light,
For she has given away her heart elsewhere;
The blessed gods in their eternal might
Have shown me in a vision, all too right;
It was Criseyde, I saw her, thus and thus.'
And he recounted all to Pandarus.

'O my Criseyde, alas, what subtle word,
What new desire, what beauty, or what art,
What anger justly caused that I incurred,
What fell experience, what guilt of heart
Robbed me of your regard? O bitter smart!
O trust, O faith! Assurance deeply tried!
Who has bereft me of my joy, Criseyde?

[135]

What shal I doon, my Pandarus, allas!
I fele now so sharpe a newe peyne,
Sin that ther is no remedie in this cas,
That bet were it I with myn hondes tweyne
My-selven slow, than alwey thus to pleyne.
For through my deeth my wo sholde han an ende,
Ther every day with lyf my-self I shende.'

Pandare answerde and seyde, 'allas the whyle
That I was born; have I not seyd er this,
That dremes many a maner man bigyle?
And why? for folk expounden hem a-mis.
How darstow seyn that fals thy lady is,
For any dreem, right for thyn owene drede?
Lat be this thought, thou canst no dremes rede.

Paraunter, ther thou dremest of this boor,
It may so be that it may signifye
Hir fader, which that old is and eek hoor,
Ayein the sonne lyth, on poynt to dye,
And she for sorwe ginneth wepe and crye,
And kisseth him, ther he lyth on the grounde;
Thus shuldestow thy dreem a-right expounde.'

19. *The Nun's Priest's Tale*

lines 62–356, with omissions

And so bifel, that in a daweninge,
As Chauntecleer among his wyves alle
Sat on his perche, that was in the halle,
And next him sat this faire Pertelote,
This Chauntecleer gan gronen in his throte,
As man that in his dreem is drecched sore.
And whan that Pertelote thus herde him rore,
She was agast, and seyde, 'O herte dere,

'What shall I do, my Pandarus, alas!
So sharp, so new, so desperate the ache,
So without remedy what has come to pass,
That it were better with these hands to take
My life than thus to suffer for her sake;
For death would end my grief and set me free,
While every day I live disgraces me.'

'Alas,' said Pandar, 'these are heavy days!
Why was I born? Haven't I always said
That dreams can fool you in a hundred ways?
And why? Because they're misinterpreted.
How dare you let such thoughts into your head
Just for a dream, just for your perturbation?
What do you know about interpretation?

'Perhaps this boar that figures in your story
Is there—it well may be—to signify
Her father Calkas, who is old and hoary;
He struggles out into the sun to die,
And she, in grief, begins to weep and cry,
And kiss him as he wallows there confounded;
That is the way your dream should be expounded.'

19. *Are Dreams Diagnostic or Prophetic?*

Now it befell, as dawn began to spring,
When Chanticleer and Pertelote and all
His wives sat perched in this poor widow's hall,
And Pertelote was next him on the perch,
This Chanticleer began to groan and lurch,
Like someone sorely troubled by a dream;
Now Pertelote, hearing him roar and scream,
Was quite aghast, and said 'O dearest heart,

What eyleth yow, to grone in this manere?
Ye been a verray sleper, fy for shame!'
And he answerde and seyde thus, 'madame,
I pray yow, that ye take it nat a-grief:
By god, me mette I was in swich meschief
Right now, that yet myn herte is sore afright.
Now god,' quod he, 'my swevene recche aright,
And keep my body out of foul prisoun!
Me mette, how that I romed up and doun
Withinne our yerde, wher-as I saugh a beste,
Was lyk an hound, and wolde han maad areste
Upon my body, and wolde han had me deed.
His colour was bitwixe yelwe and reed;
And tipped was his tail, and bothe his eres,
With blak, unlyk the remenant of his heres;
His snowte smal, with glowinge eyen tweye.
Yet of his look for fere almost I deye;
This caused me my groning, doutelees.'

'Avoy!' quod she, 'fy on yow hertelees!
Allas!' quod she, 'for, by that god above,
Now han ye lost myn herte and al my love;
I can nat love a coward, by my feith.
For certes, what so any womman seith,
We alle desyren, if it mighte be,
To han housbondes hardy, wyse, and free,
And secree, and no nigard, ne no fool,
Ne him that is agast of every tool,
Ne noon avauntour, by that god above!
How dorste ye seyn for shame unto your love,
That any thing mighte make yow aferd?
Have ye no mannes herte, and han a berd?
Allas! and conne ye been agast of swevenis?
No-thing, god wot, but vanitee, in sweven is.
Swevenes engendren of replecciouns,
And ofte of fume, and of complecciouns,
Whan humours been to habundant in a wight.
Certes this dreem, which ye han met to-night,
Cometh of the grete superfluitee

What's ailing you, to make you groan and start?
Fie, what a sleeper! What a noise to make!'
 Madam,' he said, 'I beg you not to take
Offence at it, but Lord! I had a dream
So terrible just now, I *had* to scream;
My poor heart's palpitating still, from fear!
God turn my dream to good and guard us here,
And keep my body out of durance vile!
I dreamed that roaming up and down awhile
Within our yard, I saw a kind of beast,
Much like a hound; it would have made a feast
Upon my body, would have killed me dead!
His colour was a blend of yellow and red,
His ears and tail were tipped with sable fur
Unlike the rest of him; he was a cur
With a small snout, his eyes were glowing bright.
I feel I still could almost die of fright;
This was no doubt what made me groan and swoon.'
  'For shame!' she said 'you timorous poltroon!
Alas for cowardice! By God above
You now have lost my heart and all my love.
I cannot love a coward, come what may!
And certainly, whatever women say,
We all desire—O that it might be thus!—
To have our husbands wise and generous
Hardy, discreet, no niggard yet no fool,
That boasts and then will find his courage cool
At every trifling thing! By God above,
How dared you say, for shame, and to your love,
That there was anything at all you feared?
Have you no manly heart, yet have a beard?
Alas, can dreams inspire you with such terror?
Dreams are, God knows, all vanity and error;
Dreams take their origin from a repletion
Of belly-vapours—fumes whose non-excretion
Makes for an over-abundance in the blood
Of certain 'humours' that are then in flood.
Your last night's dream was certainly a feature

Of youre rede *colera*, pardee,
Which causeth folk to dreden in here dremes
Of arwes, and of fyr with rede lemes,
Of grete bestes, that they wol hem byte,
Of contek, and of whelpes grete and lyte;
Right as the humour of malencolye
Causeth ful many a man, in sleep, to crye,
For fere of blake beres, or boles blake,
Or elles, blake develes wole hem take.
Of othere humours coude I telle also,
That werken many a man in sleep ful wo;
But I wol passe as lightly as I can.

Lo Catoun, which that was so wys a man,
Seyde he nat thus, ne do no fors of dremes?
Now, sire,' quod she, 'whan we flee fro the bemes,
For Goddes love, as tak som laxatyf;
Up peril of my soule, and of my lyf,
I counseille yow the beste, I wol nat lye,
That bothe of colere and of malencolye
Ye purge yow; and for ye shul nat tarie,
Though in this toun is noon apotecarie,
I shal my-self to herbes techen yow,
That shul ben for your hele, and for your prow;
And in our yerd tho herbes shal I finde,
The whiche han of hir propretee, by kinde,
To purgen yow binethe, and eek above.
Forget not this, for goddes owene love!
Ye been ful colerik of compleccioun.
Ware the sonne in his ascencioun
Ne fynde yow nat repleet of humours hote;
And if it do, I dar wel leye a grote,
That ye shul have a fevere terciane,
Or an agu, that may be youre bane.
A day or two ye shul have digestyves
Of wormes, er ye take your laxatyves,
Of lauriol, centaure, and fumetere,
Or elles of ellebor, that groweth there,
Of catapuce, or of gaytres beryis,

Of an excess of choler in a creature,
Red choler I say, which causes dreams of dread,
Of blood-stained arrows, fires flaming red,
Of great red beasts, making as if to fight him,
Of strife, and mongrels great and small to bite him,
Just as the black and melancholy vapours
Make many scream in sleep, and they cut capers
In terror of black bears and bulls as well,
Or of black devils haling them to Hell.

   'And there are other vapours that I know
That on a sleeping man will work their woe,
But I'll pass on as lightly as I can;
Take Cato, now, that was so wise a man,
Did he not say "Take no account of dreams"?
Now, Sir,' she said, 'on flying from the beams,
For love of God, do take a laxative!
On my soul's peril, the advice I give
Is much the best, I do not lie. I urge
You to expel both vapours with a purge
—Choler and melancholy; and, not to tarry
Because this town has no apothecary,
I shall myself instruct you in a wealth
Of herbs to guard your honour and your health,
Herbs from our very farmyard! You will find
Their natural property is to unbind,
And purge you; purge beneath and purge above.
Do not forget about it, for God's love!
Your face is choleric and shows distension;
Be careful lest the sun in his ascension
Should catch you full of vapours, hot and many;
And if it does, I dare to lay a penny
It means a bout of fever, or a breath
Of tertian ague; you may catch your death.

   'Worms, for a day or two, I'll have to give
As a digestive, then your laxative;
Centaury, fumitary, caper-spurge
And hellebore will make a splendid purge,
And then there's laurel, or the blackthorn berry,

Of erbe yve, growing in our yerd, that mery is;
Pekke hem up right as they growe, and ete hem in.
Be mery, housbond, for your fader kin!
Dredeth no dreem; I can say yow na-more.'

'Madame,' quod he, *'graunt mercy* of your lore.
But nathelees, as touching daun Catoun,
That hath of wisdom such a greet renoun,
Though that he bad no dremes for to drede,
By god, men may in olde bokes rede
Of many a man, more of auctoritee
Than ever Catoun was, so mote I thee,
That al the revers seyn of his sentence,
And han wel founden by experience,
That dremes ben significaciouns,
As wel of joye as tribulaciouns
That folk enduren in this lyf present.
Ther nedeth make of this noon argument;
The verray preve sheweth it in dede.

Oon of the gretteste auctours that men rede
Seith thus, that whylom two felawes wente
On pilgrimage, in a ful good entente;
And happed so, thay come into a toun,
Wher-as ther was swich congregacioun
Of peple, and eek so streit of herbergage
That they ne founde as muche as o cotage
In which they bothe mighte y-logged be.
Wherfor thay mosten, of necessitee,
As for that night, departen compaignye;
And ech of hem goth to his hostelrye,
And took his logging as it wolde falle.
That oon of hem was logged in a stalle,
Fer in a yerd, with oxen of the plough;
That other man was logged wel y-nough,
As was his aventure, or his fortune,
That us governeth alle as in commune.

And so bifel, that, longe er it were day,
This man mette in his bed, ther-as he lay,
How that his felawe gan up-on him calle,

Ground-ivy too, that makes our yard so merry;
Peck 'em up, just as they grow, and swallow whole;
Be merry, husband, by your father's soul!
And dread no dream; I can say nothing more.'

'Madam,' said he, 'I thank you for your lore,
But with regard to Cato, whom you name,
Whose wisdom has, no doubt, a certain fame,
Though he opined that we should take no heed
Of dreams, by God, in ancient books I read
Of many a man of more authority
Than ever Cato was, believe you me,
Who say the very opposite is true,
And have discovered by experience too
That dreams quite often give signification
As well of triumph as of tribulation,
That people undergo in this our life;
This needs no argument at all, dear wife,
The proof is all too manifest in deed.

'One of the greatest authors one can read
Says thus: there were two comrades, once, who went
On pilgrimage, sincere in their intent;
Now, as it happened, they had reached a town
Where such a throng was milling up and down,
But where there was such scant accommodation,
They could not find themselves a habitation,
No, not a cottage that could lodge them both;
And so they separated, very loath,
Under constraint of this necessity,
And each went off to find some hostelry
And lodge whatever way his luck should fall.

'The first of them found refuge in a stall
Down in a yard, with oxen and a plough;
His friend found lodging for himself somehow,
Whether by accident or destiny,
Which governs all of us, and equally.

'Now, so it happened, long ere it was day,
This fellow had a dream, and as he lay
In bed, it seemed he heard his comrade call

And seyde, "allas! for in an oxes stalle
This night I shal be mordred ther I lye.
Now help me, dere brother, er I dye;
In alle haste com to me," he sayde.
This man out of his sleep for fere abrayde;
But whan that he was wakned of his sleep,
He turned him, and took of this no keep;
Him thoughte his dreem nas but a vanitee.
Thus twyës in his sleping dremed he.
And atte thridde tyme yet his felawe
Cam, as him thoughte, and seide, "I am now slawe;
Bihold my blody woundes, depe and wyde!
Arys up erly in the morwe-tyde,
And at the west gate of the toun," quod he,
"A carte ful of dong ther shaltow see,
In which my body is hid ful prively;
Do thilke carte aresten boldely.
My gold caused my mordre, sooth to sayn;"
And tolde him every poynt how he was slayn,
With a ful pitous face, pale of hewe.
And truste wel, his dreem he fond ful trewe;
For on the morwe, as sone as it was day,
To his felawes in he took the way;
And whan that he cam to this oxes stalle,
After his felawe he bigan to calle.

  The hostiler answered him anon,
And seyde, "sire, your felawe is agon,
As sone as day he wente out of the toun."
This man gan fallen in suspecioun,
Remembring on his dremes that he mette,
And forth he goth, no lenger wolde he lette,
Unto the west gate of the toun, and fond
A dong-carte, as it were to donge lond,
That was arrayed in the same wyse
As ye han herd the dede man devyse;
And with an hardy herte he gan to crye
Vengeaunce and justice of this felonye:—
"My felawe mordred is this same night,

"Help! I am lying in a cattle-stall,
And shall to-night be murdered as I lie.
Help me, dear brother, help, or I shall die!
Come in all haste!" Such were the words he spoke;
The dreamer, lost in terror, then awoke,
But, once awake, he paid it no attention,
Turned over and dismissed it as invention;
It was a dream, he thought, a fantasy.
And twice he dreamed this dream successively.

'Yet a third time his comrade came again,
Or seemed to come, and said "I have been slain;
Look at my bloody wounds, so wide and deep!
Rise early in the morning, break your sleep,
And go to the west gate. You there shall see
A dung-cart loaded up with dung," said he,
"And in that dung my body has been hidden.
Boldly arrest that cart as you are bidden;
It was my money that they killed me for."
He told him every detail, sighing sore,
And pitiful in feature, pale of hue.

'This dream, believe me, Madam, turned out true;
For in the dawn, as soon as it was light,
He went to where his friend had spent the night,
And, when he came upon the cattle-stall,
He looked about him and began to call.
The innkeeper appearing thereupon
Quickly gave answer "Sir, your friend has gone;
He left the town a little after dawn."
The man began to feel suspicious; drawn
By memories of his dream, the western gate,
The dung-cart; off he went, he wouldn't wait,
Towards the western entry; there he found,
Seemingly on its way to dung some ground,
A dung-cart, loaded on the very plan
Described so closely by the murdered man,
And he began to shout courageously
For right and vengeance on this felony:
"My friend's been murdered in a foul attack

And in this carte he lyth gapinge upright.
I crye out on the ministres," quod he,
"That sholden kepe and reulen this citee;
Harrow! allas! her lyth my felawe slayn!"
What sholde I more un-to this tale sayn?
The peple out-sterte, and caste the cart to grounde,
And in the middel of the dong they founde
The dede man, that mordred was al newe.

O blisful god, that art so just and trewe!
Lo, how that thou biwreyest mordre alway!
Mordre wol out, that see we day by day.
Mordre is so wlatsom and abhominable
To god, that is so just and resonable,
That he ne wol nat suffre it heled be;
Though it abyde a yeer, or two, or three,
Mordre wol out, this my conclusioun.
And right anoon, ministres of that toun
Han hent the carter, and so sore him pyned,
And eek the hostiler so sore engyned,
That thay biknewe hir wikkednesse anoon,
And were an-hanged by the nekke-boon.
And therfor, faire Pertelote so dere,
By swiche ensamples olde maistow lere,
That no man sholde been to recchelees
Of dremes, for I sey thee, doutelees,
That many a dreem ful sore is for to drede.
Dame Pertelote, I sey yow trewely,
Macrobeus, that writ th'avisioun
In Affrike of the worthy Cipioun,
Affermeth dremes, and seith that they been
Warning of thinges that men after seen.

And forther-more, I pray yow loketh wel
In th'olde testament, of Daniel,
If he held dremes any vanitee.
Reed eek of Joseph, and ther shul ye see
Wher dremes ben somtyme (I sey nat alle)
Warning of thinges that shul after falle.
Loke of Egipt the king, daun Pharao,

[146]

And in that cart lies gaping on his back!
I call the authorities! Fetch the sheriff down,
Whosoever job it is to rule the town!
Alas, my friend is murdered, sent to glory!"

'What need I add to finish off this story?
People ran out and cast the cart to ground,
And in the middle of the dung they found
The murdered man; the corpse was fresh and new.

'O blessed God, that art so just and true,
Thus thou revealest murder! As we say,
"Murder will out"; we see it day by day.
Murder's so foul, so horrible a treason,
So loathsome to God's justice and His reason,
He will not suffer its concealment; true,
It may lie hidden for a year or two,
But still, *"Murder will out"*, that's my conclusion.

'All the town officers, in great confusion,
Seized on the carter and they gave him Hell,
And then they racked the innkeeper as well,
And both confessed; and then they took the wrecks
And very justly hanged them by their necks.

'So, my fair Pertelote, if you discern
The force of this example, you may learn
One never should be careless about dreams,
For undeniably, I say, it seems
That many are a sign of trouble breeding.
And, Madam, if you would enlarge your reading,
Macrobius wrote of dreams and can explain us
Visions that came to Scipio Africanus,
And he affirms that dreams can give a due
Warning of things that later on come true.

'And then there's the Old Testament—a manual
You ought to study; see *The Book of Daniel*.
Did Daniel think a dream was vanity?
Read about Joseph, too, and you will see
That many dreams—I do not say that all—
Give cognizance of what is to befall.

'Look at Lord Pharaoh, King of Egypt! Look

[147]

His bakere and his boteler also,
Wher they ne felte noon effect in dremes.
Who-so wol seken actes of sondry remes,
May rede of dremes many a wonder thing.
  Lo Cresus, which that was of Lyde king,
Mette he nat that he sat upon a tree,
Which signified he sholde anhanged be?
Lo heer Andromacha, Ectores wyf,
That day that Ector sholde lese his lyf,
She dremed on the same night biforn,
How that the lyf of Ector sholde be lorn,
If thilke day he wente in-to bataille;
She warned him, but it mighte nat availle;
He wente for to fighte nathelees,
But he was slayn anoon of Achilles.
But thilke tale is al to long to telle,
And eek it is ny day, I may nat dwelle.
Shortly I seye, as for conclusioun,
That I shal han of this avisioun
Adversitee; and I seye forther-more,
That I ne telle of laxatyves no store,
For they ben venimous, I woot it wel;
I hem defye, I love hem never a del.
  Now let us speke of mirthe, and stinte al this;
Madame Pertelote, so have I blis,
Of o thing god hath sent me large grace;
For whan I see the beautee of your face,
Ye ben so scarlet-reed about your yën,
It maketh al my drede for to dyen;
For, also siker as *In principio*,
Mulier est hominis confusio;
Madame, the sentence of this Latin is—
Womman is mannes joye and al his blis.
For whan I fele a-night your softe syde,
Al-be-it that I may nat on you ryde,
For that our perche is maad so narwe, alas!
I am so ful of joye and of solas
That I defye bothe sweven and dreem.'

At what befell his butler and his cook;
Did not their visions have a certain force?
But those who study history, of course,
Meet many dreams that set them wondering.
What about Croesus, say, the Lydian King?
He dreamed that he was sitting in a tree,
Meaning he would be hanged; it was to be.
Or take Andromache, great Hector's wife:
The day on which he was to lose his life
She dreamed of it, the very night before,
And realized that if Hector went to war
He would be lost, that fatal day, in battle.
She warned him; he dismissed it all as prattle,
And sallied forth to fight, being self-willed,
And there he met Achilles, and was killed.

'The tale is long, and somewhat overdrawn,
And anyhow it's very nearly dawn,
So let me say, in very brief conclusion,
My dream undoubtedly foretells confusion,
It bodes me ill, I say. And, furthermore,
Upon your laxatives I set no store,
For they are venomous and I defy them;
Often enough before I've suffered by them.

'Now let us speak of mirth and stop all this.
Dear Madam, as I hope for Heaven's bliss,
In one thing God has sent me plenteous grace;
For when I see the beauty of your face,
The scarlet loveliness about your eyes,
All thought of terror and confusion dies,
For it's as certain as the Creed, I know,
"Mulier est hominis confusio"
(Madam, the meaning of this Latin is
"Woman is man's delight and all his bliss")
For when at night I feel your feathery side
Albeit that I cannot take a ride,
Because our perch, alas, was made too narrow,
Delight and solace fill me to the marrow,
And I defy all visions and all dreams!'

And with that word he fley doun fro the beem,
For it was day, and eek his hennes alle;
And with a chuk he gan hem for to calle,
For he had founde a corn, lay in the yerd.
Royal he was, he was namore aferd.

And with that word, he flew down from the beams,
For it was day, and down his hens flew all,
And with a 'chuk!' he gave the troupe a call,
For he had found a seed upon the floor;
Royal he was; he was afraid no more.

20. *The Shipman's Tale*

lines 158–192

'My dere love,' quod she, 'o my daun John,
Ful lief were me this conseil for to hyde,
But out it moot, I may namore abyde.
Myn housbond is to me the worste man
That ever was, sith that the world bigan.
But sith I am a wyf, it sit nat me
To tellen no wight of our privetee,
Neither a-bedde, ne in non other place;
God shilde I sholde it tellen, for his grace!
A wyf ne shal nat seyn of hir housbonde
But al honour, as I can understonde;
Save un-to yow thus muche I tellen shal;
As help me god, he is noght worth at al
In no degree the value of a flye.
But yet me greveth most his nigardye;
And wel ye woot that wommen naturelly
Desyren thinges sixe, as wel as I.
They wolde that hir housbondes sholde be
Hardy, and wyse, and riche, and ther-to free,
And buxom to his wyf, and fresh a-bedde.
But, by that ilke lord that for us bledde,
For his honour, my-self for to arraye,
A Sonday next, I moste nedes paye
An hundred frankes, or elles am I lorn.
Yet were me lever that I were unborn
Than me were doon a sclaundre or vileinye;
And if myn housbond eek it mighte espye,

THE WORLD OF PORTRAITURE

20. *Self-Revelation of a Bonne Bourgeoise*

'O my dear love,' she answered, 'sweet Sir John,
I hate to tell you . . . O if I were stronger!
But it must out. I cannot bear it longer.
My husband is the very meanest man,
To me at any rate, since the world began.
It's unbecoming, since I am his wife,
To tell a soul about our private life,
Whether in bed or any other place,
And God forbid I sank to such disgrace!
I know a wife should only speak in honour
About her husband, or else fie upon her!
Only to you, the only one on earth,
Thus much I'll say: so help me, he's not worth
A fly upon the wall! In *no* respect,
But his worst fault is niggardly neglect.
For you must know that women naturally
Wish for six things in husbands, just like me;
They want to have their husbands (to be candid)
Sturdy and prudent, rich and open-handed,
Obedient to their wives, and fresh in bed.

But, by the Lord that died for us and bled,
By Sunday next, if I am to look smart,
And do my husband honour, I must part
With—well, a hundred francs, or I'm undone!
Far better not be born than to be one
That people slandered—said cheap things about.
Yet, if my husband were to find it out,

I nere but lost, and therfore I yow preye
Lene me this somme, or elles moot I deye.
Daun John, I seye, lene me thise hundred frankes;
Pardee, I wol nat faille yow my thankes,
If that yow list to doon that I yow praye.
For at a certein day I wol yow paye,
And doon to yow what plesance and servyce
That I may doon, right as yow list devyse.

21. THE PROLOGUE TO THE CANTERBURY TALES

The Prioress

lines 118–162

Ther was also a Nonne, a Prioresse,
That of hir smyling was ful simple and coy;
Hir gretteste ooth was but by sëynt Loy;
And she was cleped madame Eglentyne.
Ful wel she song the service divyne,
Entuned in hir nose ful semely;
And Frensh she spak ful faire and fetisly,
After the scole of Stratford atte Bowe,
For Frensh of Paris was to hir unknowe.
At mete wel y-taught was she with-alle;
She leet no morsel from hir lippes falle,
Ne wette hir fingres in hir sauce depe.
Wel coude she carie a morsel, and wel kepe,
That no drope ne fille up-on hir brest.
In curteisye was set ful muche hir lest.
Hir over lippe wyped she so clene,
That in hir coppe was no ferthing sene
Of grece, whan she dronken hadde hir draughte.
Ful semely after hir mete she raughte,

I'd be as good as lost—Ah, don't deny!
Lend me this little sum or I shall die.
Sir John, I say, lend me these hundred francs!
Trust me, I will not fail you in my thanks,
If only you'll oblige me as I say!
I'll pay you back, and you shall name the day,
And if there's anything else—some little task
That I can do for you, well, only ask . . .'

21. *Madame Eglantine*

There also was a nun, a Prioress,
Her way of smiling very simple and coy;
Her greatest oath was only 'By St. Loy!'
And she was known as Madame Eglantine.
And well she sang a service, with a fine
Intoning through her nose (as is most seemly)
And she spoke daintily in French, extremely,
After the school of Stratford-atte-Bowe.
French of the Paris kind she did not know.
She knew her table-manners one and all;
No morsel from her lips did she let fall,
Nor dipped her fingers in the sauce too deep;
Well could she carry a morsel up, and keep
The smallest drop from falling on her breast.
For courtliness she had a special zest,
And she would wipe her upper lip so clean
That not a trace of grease was to be seen
Upon the cup when she had drunk; to eat,
She reached her hand sedately for the meat;

She was so charitable and so pitous,
She wolde wepe, if that she sawe a mous
Caught in a trappe, if it were deed or bledde.
Of smale houndes had she, that she fedde
With rosted flesh, or milk and wastel-breed.
But sore weep she if oon of hem were deed,
Or if men smoot it with a yerde smerte:
And al was conscience and tendre herte.
Ful semely hir wimpel pinched was;
Hir nose tretys; hir eyen greye as glas;
Hir mouth ful smal, and ther-to softe and reed;
But sikerly she hadde a fair forheed;
It was almost a spanne brood, I trowe;
For, hardily, she was nat undergrowe.
Ful fetis was hir cloke, as I was war.
Of smal coral aboute hir arm she bar
A peire of bedes, gauded al with grene;
And ther-on heng a broche of gold ful shene,
On which ther was first write a crowned A,
And after, *Amor vincit omnia*.

22. THE PROLOGUE TO THE CANTERBURY TALES

The Wife of Bath

lines 445–476

A good Wyf was ther of bisyde Bathe,
But she was som-del deef, and that was scathe.
Of clooth-making she hadde swiche an haunt,
She passed hem of Ypres and of Gaunt.
In al the parisshe wyf ne was ther noon
That to th' offring bifore hir sholde goon;
And if ther dide, certeyn, so wrooth was she,

She was most dignified in all her dealings.
   As for her sympathies and tender feelings,
She was so charitably solicitous
She used to weep if she but saw a mouse
Caught in a trap—if it were dead or bleeding;
And she had little dogs she would be feeding
With roasted flesh, or milk, or fine white bread.
And bitterly she wept if one were dead,
Or someone took a stick to make it smart;
She was all sentiment and tender heart.
   Her veil was gathered in a seemly way,
Her nose was elegant, her eyes glass-grey;
Her mouth was very small, but soft and red;
Her forehead, certainly was fair of spread;
Her cloak, I noticed, had a graceful charm.
She wore a coral trinket on her arm,
A set of beads the gaudies tricked in green,
Whence hung a golden brooch of brightest sheen,
On which there first was graven a crowned A,
And after *Amor vincit omnia*.

22. *The Wife of Bath*

A worthy woman from beside Bath city
Was with us, somewhat deaf, which was a pity.
In making cloth she showed so great a bent
She bettered those of Ypres and of Ghent.
In all the parish, not a dame dared stir
Towards the altar steps in front of her,
And if indeed they did, so wrath was she

That she was out of alle charitee.
Hir coverchiefs ful fyne were of ground;
I dorste swere they weyeden ten pound
That on a Sonday were upon hir heed.
Hir hosen weren of fyn scarlet reed,
Ful streite y-teyd, and shoos ful moiste and newe.
Bold was hir face, and fair, and reed of hewe.
She was a worthy womman al hir lyve,
Housbondes at chirche-dore she hadde fyve,
Withouten other companye in youthe;
But therof nedeth nat to speke as nouthe.
And thryes hadde she been at Jerusalem;
She hadde passed many a straunge streem;
At Rome she hadde been, and at Boloigne,
In Galice at seint Jame, and at Coloigne.
She coude muche of wandring by the weye:
Gat-tothed was she, soothly for to seye.
Up-on an amblere esily she sat,
Y-wimpled wel, and on hir heed an hat
As brood as is a bokeler or a targe;
A foot-mantel aboute hir hipes large,
And on hir feet a paire of spores sharpe.
In felawschip wel coude she laughe and carpe.
Of remedyes of love she knew perchaunce,
For she coude of that art the olde daunce.

23. THE PROLOGUE TO THE CANTERBURY TALES

The Pardoner

lines 675–706

This pardoner hadde heer as yelow as wex,
But smothe it heng, as dooth a strike of flex;

As to be quite put out of charity.

Her kerchiefs were of finely woven ground,
I dared have sworn they weighed a good ten pound,
The ones she wore on Sunday, on her head.
Her hose were of the finest scarlet red
And gartered tight; her shoes were soft and new.
Bold was her face, handsome, and red in hue.

A worthy woman all her life, what's more,
She'd had five husbands, all at the church door,
Apart from other company in youth;
No need just now to speak of that, forsooth.
And she had thrice been to Jerusalem,
Seen many strange rivers and passed over them,
She'd been to Rome, and also to Boulogne,
St. James of Compostella, and Cologne,
And she was skilled in wandering by the way.
She had gap-teeth, set widely, truth to say
Easily on an ambling horse she sat,
Well wimpled up, and on her head a hat
As broad as is a buckler or a shield.
She had a flowing mantle that concealed
Large hips, her heels spurred sharply under that.
In company she liked to laugh and chat
And knew the remedies for love's mischances,
An art in which she knew the oldest dances.

23. *A Fund-raiser For the Church*

This Pardoner had hair as yellow as wax,
But it fell smoothly, like a hank of flax,

By ounces henge his lokkes that he hadde,
And ther-with he his shuldres overspradde;
But thinne it lay, by colpons oon and oon;
But hood, for jolitee, ne wered he noon,
For it was trussed up in his walet.
Him thoughte, he rood al of the newe jet;
Dischevele, save his cappe, he rood al bare.
Swiche glaringe eyen hadde he as an hare.
A vernicle hadde he sowed on his cappe.
His walet lay biforn him in his lappe,
Bret-ful of pardoun come from Rome al hoot.
A voys he hadde as smal as hath a goot.
No berd hadde he, ne never sholde have,
As smothe it was as it were late y-shave;
I trowe he were a gelding or a mare.
But of his craft, fro Berwik into Ware,
Ne was ther swich another pardoner.
For in his male he hadde a pilwe-beer,
Which that, he seyde, was our lady veyl:
He seyde, he hadde a gobet of the seyl
That sëynt Peter hadde, whan that he wente
Up-on the see, til Jesu Crist him hente.
He hadde a croys of latoun, ful of stones,
And in a glas he hadde pigges bones.
But with thise relikes, whan that he fond
A povre person dwelling up-on lond,
Up-on a day he gat him more moneye
Than that the person gat in monthes tweye.
And thus, with feyned flaterye and japes,
He made the person and the peple his apes.

Driblet by driblet, down behind his head,
Onto his shoulders, which it overspread;
Thinly it fell, in rat-tails, one by one.
He wore no hood upon his head, for fun;
The hood inside his wallet had been stowed,
He aimed at riding in the latest mode
(Save for a cap) disorderly and bare,
And he had glaring eye-balls, like a hare,
He'd a Veronica, sewn upon his cap.

His wallet lay before him on his lap,
Brim-full of pardons come from Rome, all hot;
He had the same small voice a goat has got.
His chin no beard had harboured, nor would harbour,
Smoother than ever chin was left by barber.
I judge he was a gelding—or a mare.
As to his trade, from Berwick down to Ware,
There was no Pardoner of equal grace,
For in his trunk he had a pillow-case,
Which, he asserted, was Our Lady's veil;
He said he had a gobbet of the sail
St. Peter had, the time when he made bold
To walk the waves, till Jesu Christ took hold.
He had a cross of metal set with stones,
And, in a glass, a rubble of pigs' bones;
Armed with these relics, any time he found
Some poor up-country parson to astound,
On one short day, in money down, he drew
More than the parson in a month or two,
And, by his flatteries and prevarication,
Made monkeys of the priest and congregation.

24. THE PROLOGUE TO THE CANTERBURY TALES

The Parson

lines 477–528, with omissions

A good man was ther of religioun,
And was a povre Persoun of a toun;
But riche he was of holy thoght and werk.
He was also a lerned man, a clerk,
That Cristes gospel trewely wolde preche;
His parisshens devoutly wolde he teche.
Benigne he was, and wonder diligent,
And in adversitee ful pacient;
And swich he was y-preved ofte sythes.
Ful looth were him to cursen for his tythes,
But rather wolde he yeven, out of doute,
Un-to his povre parisshens aboute
Of his offring, and eek of his substaunce.
He coude in litel thing han suffisaunce.
Wyd was his parisshe, and houses fer a-sonder,
But he ne lafte nat, for reyn ne thonder,
In siknes nor in meschief, to visyte
The ferreste in his parisshe, much and lyte,
To drawen folk to heven by fairnesse
By good ensample, was his bisinesse:
But it were any persone obstinat,
What-so he were, of heigh or lowe estat,
Him wolde he snibben sharply for the nones.
A bettre preest, I trowe that nowher noon is.
He wayted after no pompe and reverence,
Ne maked him a spyced conscience,
But Cristes lore, and his apostles twelve,
He taughte, and first he folwed it himselve.

24. *A Country Parson*

A holy-minded man of good renown
Was with us—the poor parson to a town;
Yet he was rich in holy thought and work;
He also was a learned man, a clerk
Who knew Christ's gospel truly, which he'd preach
Devoutly to the flock he had to teach.
Benign and wonderfully diligent,
And patient when adversity was sent
(For so he proved in much adversity).
He excommunicated nobody
For tithes unpaid—nay, rather, do not doubt—
Liked giving to poor parishioners round about
From the offertory, or from his own stuff;
For his own needs a little was enough.
  Wide was his parish, with houses far asunder,
Yet he neglected not, for rain or thunder,
In sickness or in grief, to pay a call
On the remotest, whether great or small;
His business was to show a fair behaviour
And draw men thus to Heaven and their Saviour;
Unless, indeed, a man were obstinate,
And such, whether of high or low estate,
He put to sharp rebuke, to say the least;
I think there never was a better priest;
He sought no pomp or glory in his dealings;
No scrupulosity ever spiced his feelings,
But Christ, His twelve Apostles, and their lore
He taught, but followed it himself before.

25. THE PROLOGUE TO THE CANTERBURY TALES

The Squire

lines 79–100

With him ther was his sone, a yong Squyer,
A lovyere, and a lusty bacheler,
With lokkes crulle, as they were leyd in presse.
Of twenty yeer of age he was, I gesse.
Of his stature he was of evene lengthe,
And wonderly deliver, and greet of strengthe.
And he had been somtyme in chivachye,
In Flaundres, in Artoys, and Picardye,
And born him wel, as of so litel space,
In hope to stonden in his lady grace.
Embrouded was he, as it wore a mede
Al ful of fresshe floures, whyte and rede.
Singinge he was, or floytinge, al the day;
He was as fresh as is the month of May.
Short was his goune, with sleves longe and wyde.
Wel coude he sitte on hors, and faire ryde.
He coude songes make and wel endyte,
Juste and eek daunce, and wel purtreye and wryte.
So hote he lovede, that by nightertale
He sleep namore than dooth a nightingale.
Curteys he was, lowly, and servisable,
And carf biforn his fader at the table.

25. An Accomplished Young Man

With him there was his son, a fine young Squire,
A lover and cadet, a lad of fire,
With curly locks, as if they had been pressed;
He was some twenty years of age, I guessed.
In stature he was of a moderate length,
With wonderful agility and strength.
He'd seen some service with the cavalry
In Flanders and Artois and Picardy,
And had shown well in such a little space
Of time, in hope to win his lady's grace.
He was embroidered like a meadow, bright
And full of freshest flowers, red and white.
Singing he was or fluting all the day;
He was as fresh as is the month of May.
Short was his gown; the sleeves were long and wide;
Well he knew how to sit a horse and ride.
He could make songs and poems and recite,
Knew how to joust and dance, to draw and write.
He loved so hotly that till dawn grew pale
He slept no more than does a nightingale.
Courteous he was, lowly and serviceable,
And carved to serve his father at the table.

26. THE COOK'S TALE

The Apprentice

lines 1-58

A Prentis whylom dwelled in our citee,
And of a craft of vitaillers was he;
Gaillard he was as goldfinch in the shawe,
Broun as a berie, a propre short felawe,
With lokkes blake, y-kempt ful fetisly.
Daunen he coude so wel and jolily,
That he was cleped Perkin Revelour.
He was as ful of love and paramour
As is the hyve ful of hony swete;
Wel was the wenche with him mighte mete.
At every brydale wolde he singe and hoppe,
He loved bet the tavern than the shoppe.

For whan ther any ryding was in Chepe,
Out of the shoppe thider wolde he lepe.
Til that he hadde al the sighte y-seyn,
And daunced wel, he wolde nat come ageyn.
And gadered him a meinee of his sort
To hoppe and singe, and maken swich disport.
And ther they setten steven for to mete
To pleyen at the dys in swich a strete.
For in the toune nas ther no prentys,
That fairer coude caste a paire of dys
Therfore his maister yaf him acquitance,
And bad him go with sorwe and with meschance;
And thus this joly prentis hadde his leve.
Now lat him riote al the night or leve.

And for ther is no theef with-oute a louke,
That helpeth him to wasten and to souke
Of that he brybe can or borwe may,

26. *Another*

There was a prentice living in our town
Worked in the victualling trade, and he was brown,
Brown as a berry; spruce and short he stood,
As gallant as a goldfinch in the wood.
Black were his locks and combed with fetching skill;
He danced so merrily, with such a will,
That he was known as Revelling Peterkin;
He was as full of love, as full of sin,
As hives are full of honey, and as sweet;
Lucky the wench that Peter chanced to meet.
At every wedding he would sing and hop,
And he preferred the tavern to the shop.
Whenever any pageant or procession
Came down Cheapside, good-bye to his profession!
He'd leap out of the shop to see the sight
And dance away, and not come back till night.
He gathered round him many of his sort
And made a gang for dancing, song and sport . . .
They used to make appointments where to meet
For playing dice in such and such a street,
And no apprentice had a touch so nice
As Peter, when it came to casting dice . . .

His master, then, gave Peterkin the sack
With curses, and forbade him to come back,
And so this jolly apprentice left his shop;
Now let him revel all the night, or stop.

As there's no thief without a pal or plucker
To help him to lay waste, or milk the sucker,
Whom he can bribe or borrow from at need,

Anon he sente his bed and his array
Un-to a compeer of his owne sort,
That lovede dys and revel and disport,
And hadde a wyf that heeld for countenance
A shoppe, and swyved for hir sustenance.

27. THE PROLOGUE TO THE CANTERBURY TALES

The Miller

lines 545–566

The Miller was a stout carl, for the nones,
Ful big he was of braun, and eek of bones;
That proved wel, for over-al ther he cam,
At wrastling he wolde have alwey the ram.
He was short-sholdred, brood, a thikke knarre,
Ther nas no dore that he nolde heve of harre,
Or breke it, at a renning, with his heed.
His berd as any sowe or fox was reed,
And ther-to brood, as though it were a spade.
Up-on the cop right of his nose he hade
A werte, and ther-on stood a tuft of heres,
Reed as the bristles of a sowes eres;
His nose-thirles blake were and wyde.
A swerd and bokeler bar he by his syde;
His mouth as greet was as a greet forneys.
He was a janglere and a goliardeys,
And that was most of sinne and harlotryes.
Wel coude he stelen corn, and tollen thryes;
And yet he hadde a thombe of gold, pardee.
A whyt cote and a blew hood wered he.
A baggepype wel coude he blowe and sowne,
And ther-with-al he broghte us out of towne.

He sent his bundle, and his bed indeed,
Round to an equal of the self-same sort,
As fond of dice and revelry and sport,
Whose wife kept shop; but that was only for
Display; she earned her living as a whore.

27. *A Miller*

The Miller was a chap of sixteen stone,
A great stout fellow big in brawn and bone.
They did him well; wherever he would go
He won the ram at every wrestling show.
Broad, knotty and short-shouldered, he would boast
He could heave any door off hinge and post
Or take a run and break it with his head.
His beard, like any sow or fox, was red
And broad as well, as though it were a spade;
And, at its very tip, his nose displayed
A wart, on which there stood a tuft of hair
Red as the bristles in an old sow's ear.
His nostrils were as black as they were wide.
He wore a sword and buckler at his side.
His mighty mouth was like a furnace door
A wrangler and buffoon, he had a store
Of tavern stories, filthy in the main.
His was a master-hand at stealing grain;
He felt it with his thumb, and thus he knew
Its quality and took three times his due—
A thumb of gold, by God, to gauge an oat!
He wore a hood of blue and a white coat;
He liked to play his bagpipes up and down,
And that was how he brought us out of town.

28. *The Miller's Tale*

lines 3187–3854

Whylom ther was dwellinge at Oxenford
A riche gnof, that gestes heeld to bord,
And of his craft he was a Carpenter.
With him ther was dwellinge a povre scoler,
Had lerned art, but al his fantasye
Was turned for to lerne astrologye,
And coude a certeyn of conclusiouns
To demen by interrogaciouns,
If that men axed him in certein houres,
Whan that men sholde have droghte or elles shoures,
Or if men axed him what sholde bifalle
Of every thing, I may nat rekene hem alle.

  This clerk was cleped hende Nicholas;
Of derne love he coude and of solas;
And ther-to he was sleigh and ful privee,
And lyk a mayden meke for to see.
A chambre hadde he in that hostelrye
Allone, with-outen any companye,
Ful fetisly y-dight with herbes swote;
And he him-self as swete as is the rote
Of licorys, or any cetewale.
His Almageste and bokes grete and smale,
His astrelabie, longinge for his art,
His augrim-stones layen faire a-part
On shelves couched at his beddes heed:
His presse y-covered with a falding reed.
And al above ther lay a gay sautrye,
On which he made a nightes melodye

THE STUDENT WORLD

28. *The Miller's Tale*

Some time ago there was a rich old codger
Who lived at Oxford and who took a lodger.
The fellow was a carpenter by trade,
His lodger a poor student who had made
Some studies in the Arts, but all his fancy
Turned to astrology and geomancy,
And he could deal with certain propositions
About the weather, gauging the conditions
When asked about them at the proper hours,
And tell you if there would be drought, or showers,
Or prophecy things likely to befall
In given cases—I can't count them all.

This lad was known as Nicholas the Gallant,
And making love in secret was his talent,
For he was very close and sly, and took
Advantage of his meek and girlish look.
He rented a small chamber in the kip
All by himself, without companionship.
He decked it charmingly with herbs and fruit,
And he himself was sweeter than the root
Of liquorice, or any other herb.

His astronomic text-books were superb;
He had an astrolabe to suit his art
And calculating counters set apart
On handy shelves that stood above his bed.
His press was curtained coarsely and in red;
Above it lay a harp or psaltery,
On which, at night, he made such melody,

So swetely, that al the chambre rong;
And *Angelus ad virginem* he song;
And after that he song the kinges note;
Ful often blessed was his mery throte.
And thus this swete clerk his tyme spente
After his freendes finding and his rente.

This Carpenter had wedded newe a wyf
Which that he lovede more than his lyf;
Of eightetene yeer she was of age.
Jalous he was, and heeld hir narwe in cage,
For she was wilde and yong, and he was old,
And demed him-self ben lyk a cokewold.
He knew nat Catoun, for his wit was rude,
That bad man sholde wedde his similitude.
Men sholde wedden after hir estaat,
For youthe and elde is often at debaat.
But sith that he was fallen in the snare,
He moste endure, as other folk, his care.

Fair was this yonge wyf, and ther-with-al
As any wesele hir body gent and smal.
A ceynt she werede barred al of silk,
A barmclooth eek as whyt as morne milk
Up-on hir lendes, ful of many a gore.
Whyt was hir smok and brouded al bifore
And eek bihinde, on hir coler aboute,
Of col-blak silk, with-inne and eek with-oute.
The tapes of hir whyte voluper
Were of the same suyte of hir coler;
Hir filet brood of silk, and set ful hye:
And sikerly she hadde a likerous yë.
Ful smale y-pulled were hir browes two,
And tho were bent, and blake as any sloo.
She was ful more blisful on to see
Than is the newe pere-jonette tree;
And softer than the wolle is of a wether.
And by hir girdel heeng a purs of lether
Tasseld with silk, and perled with latoun.
In al this world, to seken up and doun,

So sweetly too, that all the chamber rang.
It was *The Virgin's Angelus* he sang,
And after that he sang *King William's Note*,
And people often blessed his merry throat;
And that was how this charming scholar spent
His time, and money which his friends had sent.

   This carpenter had married a new wife
Not long before, and loved her more than life.
She was a girl of eighteen years of age;
Jealous he was and kept her in the cage,
For he was old and she was wild and young;
He thought himself quite likely to be stung.
He knew not—having no Cato on his shelves—
That men should marry someone like themselves;
A man should pick an equal for his mate;
Youth and old age are often in debate.
His wits were dull, he'd fallen in the snare,
And had to bear his cross as others bear.

   She was a fair young wife, her body as slender
As any weasel's, and as soft and tender;
She used to wear a girdle of striped silk;
Her apron was as white as morning milk
Over her loins, all gusseted and pleated.
White was her smock; embroidery repeated
Its pattern on the collar, front and back,
Inside and out; it was of silk, and black.
The tapes and ribbons of her milky mutch
Were made to match her collar to a touch;
She wore a broad silk fillet rather high,
And certainly she had a lecherous eye.
And she had plucked her eyebrows into bows;
Slenderly arched, they were, and black as sloes;
And a more truly blissful sight to see
She was than blossom on a cherry-tree,
And softer than the wool upon a wether;
And by her girdle hung a purse of leather
Tasseled with silk and silver droplets, pearled;
If you went seeking up and down the world

There nis no man so wys, that coude thenche
So gay a popelote, or swich a wenche.
Ful brighter was the shyning of hir hewe
Than in the tour the noble y-forged newe.
But of hir song, it was as loude and yerne
As any swalwe sittinge on a berne.
Ther-to she coude skippe and make game,
As any kide or calf folwinge his dame.
Hir mouth was swete as bragot or the meeth,
Or hord of apples leyd in hey or heeth.
Winsinge she was, as is a joly colt,
Long as a mast, and upright as a bolt.
A brooch she baar up-on hir lowe coler,
As brood as is the bos of a bocler.
Hir shoes were laced on hir legges hye;
She was a prymerole, a pigges-nye
For any lord to leggen in his bedde,
Or yet for any good yeman to wedde.

Now sire, and eft sire, so bifel the cas,
That on a day this hende Nicholas
Fil with this yonge wyf to rage and pleye,
Whyl that hir housbond was at Oseneye,
As clerkes ben ful subtile and ful queynte;
And prively he caughte hir by the queynte,
And seyde, 'y-wis, but if ich have my wille,
For derne love of thee, lemman, I spille.'
And heeld hir harde by the haunche-bones,
And seyde, 'lemman, love me al at-ones,
Or I wol dyen, also god me save!'
And she sprong as a colt doth in the trave,
And with hir heed she wryed faste awey,
And seyde, 'I wol nat kisse thee, by my fey,
Why, lat be,' quod she, 'lat be, Nicholas,
Or I wol crye out "harrow" and "allas."
Do wey your handes for your curteisye!'

This Nicholas gan mercy for to crye,
And spak so faire, and profred hir so faste,
That she hir love him graunted atte laste,

The wisest man you met would have to wrench
His fancy to imagine such a wench;
And her complexion had a brighter tint
Than a new florin from the Royal Mint.
As to her song, it was as loud and quick
As any swallow's chirping on a rick;
And she would skip or play some game or other
Like any kid or calf behind its mother.
Her mouth was sweet as mead or honey, say
A hoard of apples, laid in heath or hay.
Skittish she was, as jolly as a colt,
Tall as a mast and straighter than a bolt
Out of a bow; her collaret revealed
A brooch as big as boss upon a shield;
High shoes she wore and laced them to the top;
She was a daisy, O a lollipop
For any nobleman to take to bed,
Or honest man of yeoman stock to wed.

  Now Gentlemen, the Gallant Nicholas
One day began to romp and make a pass
At this young wife; it happened, let me say,
The carpenter was out, down Osney way;
Students are sly, and, giving way to whim,
He made a grab and caught her by the quim,
And said 'Let's love in secret, you and I!
If I dont' have you, darling, I shall die!'
He held her haunches hard and then he said
'O love-me-all-at-once or I am dead!'
She gave a spring, just like a skittish colt
Boxed in a shoeing-frame, and with a holt
Managed in time to wrench her head away.
And said 'Give over, Nicholas, I say!
No, I won't kiss you! Stop it, let me go,
Or I shall scream and let the neighbours know!
Where are your manners? Take away your paws!'

  This Nicholas began to plead his cause,
And spoke so fair in proffering what he could,
That in the end she promised him she would,

[175]

And swoor hir ooth, by seint Thomas of Kent,
That she wol been at his comandement,
Whan that she may hir leyser wel espye.
'Myn housbond is so ful of jalousye,
That but ye wayte wel and been privee,
I woot right wel I nam but deed,' quod she.
'Ye moste been ful derne, as in this cas.'

'Nay ther-of care thee noght,' quod Nicholas,
'A clerk had litherly biset his whyle,
But-if he coude a carpenter bigyle.'
And thus they been acorded and y-sworn
To wayte a tyme, as I have told biforn.
Whan Nicholas had doon thus everydeel,
And thakked hir aboute the lendes weel,
He kist hir swete, and taketh his sautrye,
And pleyeth faste, and maketh melodye.

Than fil it thus, that to the parish-chirche,
Cristes owne werkes for to wirche,
This gode wyf wente on an haliday;
Hir forheed shoon as bright as any day,
So was it wasshen whan she leet hir werk.

Now was ther of that chirche a parish-clerk,
The which that was y-cleped Absolon.
Crul was his heer, and as the gold it shoon,
And strouted as a fanne large and brode;
Ful streight and even lay his joly shode.
His rode was reed, his eyen greye as goos;
With Powles window corven on his shoos,
In hoses rede he wente fetisly.
Y-clad he was ful smal and proprely,
Al in a kirtel of a light wachet;
Ful faire and thikke been the poyntes set.
And ther-up-on he hadde a gay surplys
As whyt as is the blosme up-on the rys.
A mery child he was, so god me save,
Wel coude he laten blood and clippe and shave,
And make a chartre of lond or acquitaunce.
In twenty manere coude he trippe and daunce

Swearing she'd love him, with a solemn promise
To be at his disposal, by St. Thomas,
When she could spy an opportunity;
'My husband is so full of jealousy,
Unless you watch your step and hold your breath,
I know for certain it will be my death,'
She said, 'so just you keep it under your hat!'
'O never mind about a thing like that,
Idle would be the scholar who couldn't stir
His wits enough to fool a carpenter.'
And so they both agreed to it and swore
To watch their chance, as I have said before.
When things were all arranged as they thought fit,
And Nicholas had stroked her loins a bit
And kissed her sweetly, he took down his harp,
And played away, a merry tune and sharp.

It happened later she went off to church,
This worthy wife, one holy day, to search
Her conscience and to do the works of Christ;
She put her work aside, for it sufficed;
Her forehead shone like day—it made its mark.

Now all this time there was a parish clerk
Serving the church, whose name was Absalon;
His hair was curly and like gold it shone;
Large as a fan it sprouted upwards, starting
To right and left in an accomplished parting.
His face was red, his eyes were grey as goose,
His shoes cut out in tracery, as in use
In Paul's cathedral, and upon his feet
His hose showed scarlet through, and all was neat
And proper. In a jacket of light blue,
Pointed and thickly tagged with laces too
He went, and wore a surplice, which was gay
And white as any blossom on the spray.
God bless my soul, he was a merry knave!
He knew how to let blood, cut hair and shave
And draw up legal deeds; at other whiles
He used to dance in twenty different styles

After the scole of Oxenforde tho,
And with his legges casten to and fro,
And pleyen songes on a small rubible;
Ther-to he song som-tyme a loud quinible;
And as wel coude he pleye on his giterne.
In al the toun nas brewhous ne taverne
That he ne visited with his solas,
Ther any gaylard tappestere was.
But sooth to seyn, he was somdel squaymous
Of farting, and of speche daungerous.

   This Absolon, that jolif was and gay,
Gooth with a sencer on the haliday,
Sensinge the wyves of the parish faste;
And many a lovely look on hem he caste,
And namely on this carpenteres wyf.
To loke on hir him thoughte a mery lyf,
She was so propre and swete and likerous.
I dar wel seyn, if she had been a mous,
And he a cat, he wolde hir hente anon.

   This parish-clerk, this joly Absolon,
Hath in his herte swich a love-longinge,
That of no wyf ne took he noon offringe;
For curteisye, he seyde, he wolde noon.
The mone, whan it was night, ful brighte shoon,
And Absolon his giterne hath y-take,
For paramours, he thoghte for to wake.
And forth he gooth, jolif and amorous,
Til he cam to the carpenteres hous
A litel after cokkes hadde y-crowe;
And dressed him up by a shot-windowe
That was up-on the carpenteres wal.
He singeth in his vois gentil and smal,
'Now, dere lady, if thy wille be,
I preye yow that ye wol rewe on me,'
Ful wel acordaunt to his giterninge.
This carpenter awook, and herde him singe,
And spak un-to his wyf, and seyde anon,
'What! Alison! herestow nat Absolon

[178]

(After the school in vogue at Oxford then,
With legs cast forward, round and back again).
He played a two-stringed fiddle, did it proud,
And sang a high falsetto rather loud,
And he was just as good on the guitar;
There was no public-house in town or bar
He didn't visit with his merry face,
If there were saucy barmaids round the place.
He was a little squeamish in the matter
Of farting, and satirical in chatter.

   This Absalon, so jolly in his ways,
Would bear the censer round on holy days
Censing the parish wives; and he would cast
Many a love-lorn look as he went past,
Especially at the carpenter's young wife;
Looking at her would make a happy life,
She was so neat and sweet and lecherous;
And I dare say if she had been a mouse
And he a cat, she'd have been pounced upon.

   In taking the collection, Absalon
Would find his heart was set in such a whirl
Of love, he would take nothing from a girl,
For courtesy (he said); it wasn't right.

   One evening when the moon was shining bright
He upped with his guitar to make his tours
Around the town, and look for paramours.
Flighty and amorous away he strode;
At last he reached the carpenter's abode
A little after cock-crow, took his stand
Beside the casement window, close at hand,
(It was set low upon the cottage face)
And started singing softly and with grace
    Now dearest lady, if thy pleasure be
    In thoughts of love, think tenderly on me!
On his guitar he plucked a tuneful string.

   This carpenter awoke and heard him sing
And, turning to his wife, said 'Alison!
Wife! Do you hear him? There goes Absalon

That chaunteth thus under our boures wal?'
And she answerde hir housbond ther-with-al,
'Yis, god wot, John, I here it every-del.'

This passeth forth; what wol ye bet than wel?
Fro day to day this joly Absolon
So woweth hir, that him is wo bigon.
He waketh al the night and al the day;
He kempte hise lokkes brode, and made him gay;
He woweth hir by menes and brocage,
And swoor he wolde been hir owne page;
He singeth, brokkinge as a nightingale;
He sente hir piment, meeth, and spyced ale,
And wafres, pyping hote out of the glede;
And for she was of toune, he profred mede.
For som folk wol ben wonnen for richesse,
And som for strokes, and som for gentillesse.

Somtyme, to shewe his lightnesse and maistrye,
He pleyeth Herodes on a scaffold hye.
But what availleth him as in this cas?
She loveth so this hende Nicholas,
That Absolon may blowe the bukkes horn;
He ne hadde for his labour but a scorn:
And thus she maketh Absolon hir ape,
And al his ernest turneth til a jape.
Ful sooth is this proverbe, it is no lye,
Men seyn right thus, 'alwey the nye slye
Maketh the ferre leve to be looth.'
For though that Absolon be wood or wrooth,
By-cause that he fer was from hir sighte,
This nye Nicholas stood in his lighte.

Now bere thee wel, thou hende Nicholas!
For Absolon may waille and singe 'allas.'
And so bifel it on a Saterday,
This carpenter was goon til Osenay;
And hende Nicholas and Alisoun
Acorded been to this conclusioun,
That Nicholas shal shapen him a wyle
This sely jalous housbond to bigyle;

Chanting away against our chamber wall!'
And she replied, 'Yes, John, I hear it all.'
If she thought more of it she didn't tell.
So things went on; what's better than 'All's well'?

   From day to day this jolly Absalon
Wooing away, became quite woe-begone;
He lay awake all night and all the day,
Combed his thick locks and tried to pass for gay,
Wooed her by go-between and wooed by proxy,
Swore to be page and servant to his doxy,
Trilled and rouladed like a nightingale,
Sent her sweet wine and mead and spicy ale,
And wafers piping hot and jars of honey,
And, as she lived in town, he offered money;
For some are won by money and good eating,
And some are won by kindness, some by beating.

   Once, in the hope his talent might engage
Her heart, he acted Herod on the stage.
What was the good? Were he as bold as brass,
She was in love with Gallant Nicholas;
However Absalon might blow his horn
His labour earned him nothing but her scorn.
She looked upon him as her private ape
And held his earnest wooing all a jape.
There is a proverb—and it is no lie—
You'll often hear repeated: '*Nigh and Sly
Defeats the Fair and Square who isn't there*'.
For much as Absalon might tear his hair,
And rage at being seldom in her sight,
Nicholas, nigh and sly, was in his light.
Now show your paces, Nicholas the Spark!
And leave lamenting to the parish clerk.

   And so it happened that one Saturday
When the old carpenter was safe away
At Osney, Nicholas and Alison
Agreed at last in what was to be done;
Nicholas was to shape a wily plan
To lull suspicions in her foolish man,

And if so be the game wente aright,
She sholde slepen in his arm al night,
For this was his desyr and hir also.
And right anon, with-outen wordes mo,
This Nicholas no lenger wolde tarie,
But doth ful softe un-to his chambre carie
Bothe mete and drinke for a day or tweye,
And to hir housbonde bad hir for to seye,
If that he axed after Nicholas,
She sholde seye she niste where he was,
Of al that day she saugh him nat with yë;
She trowed that he was in maladye,
For, for no cry, hir mayde coude him calle;
He nolde answere, for no-thing that mighte falle.

This passeth forth al thilke Saterday,
That Nicholas stille in his chambre lay,
And eet and sleep, or dide what him leste,
Til Sonday, that the sonne gooth to reste.

This sely carpenter hath greet merveyle
Of Nicholas, or what thing mighte him eyle,
And seyde, 'I am adrad, by seint Thomas,
It stondeth nat aright with Nicholas.
God shilde that he deyde sodeynly!
This world is now ful tikel, sikerly;
I saugh to-day a cors y-born to chirche
That now, on Monday last, I saugh him wirche.

Go up,' quod he un-to his knave anoon,
'Clepe at his dore, or knokke with a stoon,
Loke how it is, and tel me boldely.'

This knave gooth him up ful sturdily,
And at the chambre-dore, whyl that he stood,
He cryde and knokked as that he were wood:—
'What! how! what do ye, maister Nicholay?
How may ye slepen al the longe day?'

But al for noght, he herde nat a word;
An hole he fond, ful lowe up-on a bord,
Ther as the cat was wont in for to crepe;
And at that hole he looked in ful depe,

And if so be the trick worked out all right
She'd lie in Nicholas's arms all night,
For that was his desire and hers as well;
So, even quicker than it takes to tell,
Young Nicholas, who simply couldn't wait,
Went to his room on tiptoe with a plate
Of food and drink, enough to last a day
Or two, and Alison was told to say,
In case her husband asked for Nicholas,
That she had no idea where he was,
She hadn't even set eyes on him all day,
She thought he might be ill, she couldn't say;
And more than once the maid had given a call
And shouted, but no answer came at all.

So things went on the whole of Saturday
Without a sound from Nicholas, who lay
Upstairs, and ate or slept as pleased him best,
Till Sunday when the sun went down to rest.

This foolish carpenter was lost in wonder
At Nicholas; what could have got him under?
He said 'I can't help thinking, by the Mass,
Things can't be going right with Nicholas;
What if he took and died? God guard his ways!
A ticklish place, the world is, nowadays.
I saw a corpse this morning borne to kirk,
That only Monday last I saw at work.
Run up,' he told the serving-lad, 'be quick,
Shout at his door or knock it with a brick.
Take a good look and tell me how he fares.'
The serving-boy went sturdily upstairs
Stopped at the door, and, standing there, the lad
Shouted away and, hammering like mad,
Cried 'Ho! What's up? Hi! Master Nicholay!
How can you lie asleep up there all day?'

But all for nought; he didn't hear a soul.
He found a broken panel with a hole
Right at the bottom, useful to the cat
For creeping through; he took a look through that

And at the laste he hadde of him a sighte.
This Nicholas sat gaping ever up-righte,
As he had kyked on the newe mone.
Adoun he gooth, and tolde his maister sone
In what array he saugh this ilke man.

This carpenter to blessen him bigan,
And seyde, 'help us, seinte Frideswyde!
A man woot litel what him shal bityde.
This man is falle, with his astromye,
In som woodnesse or in som agonye;
I thoghte ay wel how that it sholde be!
Men sholde nat knowe of goddes privetee.
Ye, blessed be alwey a lewed man,
That noght but only his bileve can!
So ferde another clerk with astromye;
He walked in the feeldes for to prye
Up-on the sterres, what ther sholde bifalle,
Til he was in a marle-pit y-falle;
He saugh nat that. But yet, by seint Thomas,
Me reweth sore of hende Nicholas.
He shal be rated of his studying,
If that I may, by Jesus, hevene king!

Get me a staf, that I may underspore,
Whyl that thou, Robin, hevest up the dore.
He shal out of his studying, as I gesse'—
And to the chambre-dore he gan him dresse.
His knave was a strong carl for the nones,
And by the haspe he haf it up atones;
In-to the floor the dore fil anon.
This Nicholas sat ay as stille as stoon,
And ever gaped upward in-to the eir.
This carpenter wende he were in despeir,
And hente him by the sholdres mightily,
And shook him harde, and cryde spitously,
What! Nicholay! what, how! what! loke adoun!
Awake, and thenk on Cristes passioun;

And so at last, by peering through the crack,
He saw the scholar gaping on his back,
As if he'd caught a glimpse of the new moon.
Down went the boy and told his master soon
About the state in which he'd found the man.
On hearing this the carpenter began
To cross himself and said 'St. Frideswide bless us!
We little know what's coming to distress us;
The man has fallen with his "astromy"
Into a fit, or lunacy, maybe.
I always thought that was how it would go;
God has some secrets that we shouldn't know;
How blessed are the simple, aye, indeed,
That only know enough to say their Creed!
Happened just so with such another student
Of astromy; and he was so imprudent
As to stare upwards as he crossed a field,
Busy foreseeing what the stars revealed,
And what should happen but he fell down flat
Into a marl-pit. He didn't foresee that!
By all the Saints we've reached a sorry pass;
I can't help worrying for Nicholas.
He shall be scolded for his studying,
If I know how to scold, by Christ the King!
Give me a staff to prise against the floor;
Robin, just heave your shoulder to the door,
We'll shake the study out of him, I guess!'

The pair of them began to heave and press
Against the door; happened the lad was strong
And so it didn't take them very long
To heave it off its hinges: down it came.

Still as a stone lay Nicholas, with the same
Expression, gaping upwards into air.
The carpenter supposed it was despair
And shook him by the shoulders with a stout
And mighty shake, accompanied by a shout:
'What, Nicholas! Hey! Look down! Is that the fashion
To act? Wake up and think upon Christ's passion!

I crouche thee from elves and fro wightes!'
Ther-with the night-spel seyde he anon-rightes
On foure halves of the hous aboute,
And on the threshfold of the dore with-oute:—
   'Jesu Crist, and sëynt Benedight,
   Blesse this hous from every wikked wight,
   For nightes verye, the white *pater-noster!*—
   Where wentestow, seynt Petres soster?'
And atte laste this hende Nicholas
Gan for to syke sore, and seyde, 'allas!
Shal al the world be lost eftsones now?'

   This carpenter answerde, 'what seystow?
What! thenk on god, as we don, men that swinke.'

   This Nicholas answerde, 'fecche me drinke;
And after wol I speke in privetee
Of certeyn thing that toucheth me and thee;
I wol telle it non other man, certeyn.'

   This carpenter goth doun, and comth ageyn,
And broghte of mighty ale a large quart;
And whan that ech of hem had dronke his part,
This Nicholas his dore faste shette,
And doun the carpenter by him he sette.

   He seyde, 'John, myn hoste lief and dere,
Thou shalt up-on thy trouthe swere me here,
That to no wight thou shalt this conseil wreye;
For it is Cristes conseil that I seye,
And if thou telle it man, thou are forlore;
For this vengaunce thou shalt han therfore,
That if thou wreye me, thou shalt be wood!'
'Nay, Crist forbede it, for his holy blood!'
Quod tho this sely man, 'I nam no labbe,
Ne, though I seye, I nam nat lief to gabbe.
Sey what thou wolt, I shal it never telle
To child ne wyf, by him that harwed helle!'

   'Now John,' quod Nicholas, 'I wol nat lye;
I have y-founde in myn astrologye,
As I have loked in the mone bright,
That now, a Monday next, at quarter-night,

I sign you with the cross from elves and sprites!'
And he began the spell for use at nights
In all four corners of the room and out
Across the threshold too and round about:
>   *Jesus Christ and Benedict Sainted*
>   *Bless this house from creature tainted,*
>   *Drive away Night-Hags, white Pater Noster!*
>   *Where have you been, St. Peter's soster?*

And in the end the gallant Nicholas
Began to sigh, and 'Must it come to pass?'
He said 'Must all the world be cast away?'
The carpenter replied 'What's that you say?
Put trust in God, as we do, working men.'
Nicholas answered 'Fetch some liquor then,
And afterwards, in strictest secrecy,
I'll speak of something touching you and me,
But not another soul may know, that's plain.'

This carpenter went down and came again
Bringing some powerful ale—a largeish quart;
When each had had his share of this support,
Young Nicholas got up and shut the door
And, sitting down beside him as before,
Said to the carpenter 'Now, John, my dear
And excellent host, swear on your honour here
Not to repeat a syllable I say,
For here are Christ's intentions, to betray
Which to a soul puts you among the lost,
And vengeance for it at a bitter cost
Shall fall on you; you shall be driven mad!'
'Christ and His holy blood forbid it, lad!'
The silly fellow answered, 'I'm no blab,
Though I should say it, I'm not given to gab,
Say what you like, for I will never tell
Man, woman or child, by Him that harrowed Hell!'
'Now, John,' said Nicholas, 'believe you me,
I have found out by my astrology
And gazing at the moon when it was bright,
That Monday next, a quarter way through night,

Shal falle a reyn and that so wilde and wood,
That half so greet was never Noës flood.
This world,' he seyde, 'in lasse than in an hour
Shal al be dreynt, so hidous is the shour;
Thus shal mankynde drenche and lese hir lyf.'

This carpenter answerde, 'allas, my wyf!
And shal she drenche? allas! myn Alisoun!'
For sorwe of this he fil almost adoun,
And seyde, 'is ther no remedie in this cas?'

'Why, yis, for gode,' quod hende Nicholas,
'If thou wolt werken after lore and reed;
Thou mayst nat werken after thyn owene heed.
For thus seith Salomon, that was ful trewe,
"Werk al by conseil, and thou shalt nat rewe."
And if thou werken wolt by good conseil,
I undertake, with-outen mast and seyl,
Yet shal I saven hir and thee and me.
Hastow nat herd how saved was Noë,
Whan that our lord had warned him biforn
That al the world with water sholde be lorn?'

'Yis,' quod this carpenter, 'ful yore ago.'

'Hastow nat herd,' quod Nicholas, 'also
The sorwe of Noë with his felawshipe,
Er that he mighte gete his wyf to shipe?
Him had be lever, I dar wel undertake,
At thilke tyme, than alle hise wetheres blake,
That she hadde had a ship hir-self allone.
And ther-fore, wostou what is best to done?
This asketh haste, and of an hastif thing
Men may nat preche or maken tarying.

Anon go gete us faste in-to this in
A kneding-trogh, or elles a kimelin,
For ech of us, but loke that they be large,
In whiche we mowe swimme as in a barge.
And han ther-inne vitaille suffisant
But for a day; fy on the remenant!
The water shal aslake and goon away
Aboute pryme up-on the nexte day.

Rain is to fall in torrents—such a scud
It will be twice as bad as Noah's Flood.
This world' he said 'in just about an hour,
Will all be drowned, it's such a hideous shower,
And all mankind, with total loss of life.'
   The carpenter exclaimed 'Alas, my wife!
My little Alison! Is she to drown?'
And in his grief he almost tumbled down,
And said 'Is there no remedy for this?'
'Thanks be to God,' said Nicholas 'there is,
If you will do exactly as I say,
And don't go thinking up some other way.
In wise old Solomon you'll find the verse
"Who takes advice will never fare the worse",
And so if good advice is to prevail,
I undertake, with neither mast nor sail,
To save her yet, and save myself and you;
Haven't you heard how Noah was saved too,
When God forewarned him, and his sons and daughters,
That all the world would sink beneath the waters?'
'Yes . . .' said the carpenter, 'a long time back.'
'Haven't you heard' said Nicholas, 'what a black
Business it was, when Noah tried to whip
His wife, who wouldn't come, on board the ship?
He'd have been better pleased, I'll undertake,
With all that weather just about to break,
If she had had a vessel of her own.
What shall we do, now? For we can't postpone
The thing, it calls for haste as I was saying,
It's coming soon; no preaching, no delaying.
I want you now, at once, to hurry off
And fetch a shallow tub or kneading-trough,
For each of us; but see that they are large,
And such as we can float in, like a barge;
And have them loaded with sufficient victual
To last a day—we only need a little.
The waters will abate and flow away
Round nine o'clock upon the following day.

But Robin may nat wite of this, thy knave,
Ne eek thy mayde Gille I may nat save;
Axe nat why, for though thou aske me,
I wol nat tellen goddes privetee.
Suffiseth thee, but if thy wittes madde,
To han as greet a grace as Noë hadde.
Thy wyf shal I wel saven, out of doute,
Go now thy wey, and speed thee heer-aboute.

 But whan thou hast, for hir and thee and me,
Y-geten us thise kneding-tubbes three,
Than shaltow hange hem in the roof ful hye,
That no man of our purveyaunce spye.
And whan thou thus hast doon as I have seyd,
And hast our vitaille faire in hem y-leyd,
And eek an ax, to smyte the corde atwo
When that the water comth, that we may go,
And broke an hole an heigh, up-on the gable,
Unto the gardin-ward, over the stable,
That we may frely passen forth our way
Whan that the grete shour is goon away—
Than shaltow swimme as myrie, I undertake,
As doth the whyte doke after hir drake.
Than wol I clepe, "how! Alison! how! John!
Be myrie, for the flood wol passe anon."
And thou wolt seyn, "hayl, maister Nicholay!
Good morwe, I se thee wel, for it is day."
And than shul we be lordes al our lyf
Of al the world, as Noë and his wyf.

 But of o thyng I warne thee ful right,
Be wel avysed, on that ilke night
That we ben entred in-to shippes bord,
That noon of us ne speke nat a word,
Ne clepe, ne crye, but been in his preyere;
For it is goddes owne heste dere.

 Thy wyf and thou mote hange fer a-twinne,
For that bitwixe yow shal be no sinne
No more in looking than ther shal in dede;
This ordinance is seyd, go, god thee spede!

[190]

Robin, the lad, mayn't know of this, poor knave,
Nor Jill the maid; these two I cannot save;
Don't ask me why; and even if you do
I can't disclose God's secret thoughts to you;
You should be satisfied, unless you're mad,
To find as great a grace as Noah had.
And I will save your wife, you needn't doubt it;
Now off you go, and hurry up about it.

'And when the tubs have been collected—three—
That's one for her, and for yourself, and me,
Then hang them in the roof below the thatching,
That no one may discover what we're hatching.
When you have finished doing what I said,
And stowed the victuals in them overhead,
Also an axe to hack the ropes apart,
That, when the water rises, we may start,
And, lastly, when you've broken out the gable,
The garden one, that's just above the stable,
So that we may cast free without delay
After the mighty shower has passed away,
You'll swim as merrily, I undertake,
As any lily-white duck behind her drake.
And I'll call out "Hey, Alison! Hey, John!
Cheer yourselves up! The flood will soon have gone."
And you'll shout back "Hail, Master Nicholay!
Good morning! I can see you well, it's day!"
We shall be lords for all the rest of life
Of all the world, like Noah and his wife.

'One thing I warn you of; it's only right;
We must be very careful on the night,
Once we have safely managed to embark,
To hold our tongues and utter no remark,
No cry, no call; for we must fall to prayer;
This is the Lord's dear will, so have a care.
Your wife and you must lie some way apart,
For there must be no sin before we start,
No more in longing looks than in the deed.
Those are your orders. Off you go! God speed!

Tomorwe at night, whan men ben alle aslepe,
In-to our kneding-tubbes wol we crepe,
And sitten ther, abyding goddes grace.
Go now thy wey, I have no lenger space
To make of this no lenger sermoning.
Men seyn thus, "send the wyse, and sey no-thing;"
Thou art so wys, it nedeth thee nat teche;
Go, save our lyf, and that I thee biseche.'

This sely carpenter goth forth his wey.
Ful ofte he seith 'allas' and 'weylawey,'
And to his wyf he tolde his privetee;
And she was war, and knew it bet than he,
What al this queynte cast was for to seye.
But nathelees she ferde as she wolde deye,
And seyde, 'allas! go forth thy wey anon,
Help us to scape, or we ben lost echon;
I am thy trewe verray wedded wyf;
Go, dere spouse, and help to save our lyf.'

Lo! which a greet thyng is affeccioun!
Men may dye of imaginacioun,
So depe may impressioun be take.
This sely carpenter biginneth quake;
Him thinketh verraily that he may see
Noës flood come walwing as the see
To drenchen Alisoun, his hony dere.
He wepeth, weyleth, maketh sory chere,
He syketh with ful many a sory swogh.
He gooth and geteth him a kneding-trogh,
And after that a tubbe and a kimelin,
And prively he sente hem to his in,
And heng hem in the roof in privetee.
His owne hand he made laddres three,
To climben by the ronges and the stalkes
Un-to the tubbes hanginge in the balkes,
And hem vitailled, bothe trogh and tubbe,
With breed and chese, and good ale in a jubbe,
Suffysinge right y-nogh as for a day.
But er that he had maad al this array,

Tomorrow night, when everyone's asleep,
We'll all go quietly upstairs and creep
Into our tubs, awaiting Heaven's grace;
And now be off. No time to put the case
At greater length, no time to sermonise;
The proverb says "Say nothing, send the wise."
You are so wise there is no need to teach you;
Go, save our lives for us, as I beseech you.'

This silly carpenter then went his way
Muttering to himself 'Alas the day!'
And told his wife in strictest secrecy.
She was aware, far more indeed than he,
What this strange stratagem might have in sight,
But she pretended to be dead with fright;
'Alas!' she said 'whatever it may cost,
Hurry and help or we shall all be lost.
I am your honest, true and wedded wife,
Dear husband, go, and help to save our life!'

How fancy throws us into perturbation!
People can die of mere imagination,
So deep is the impression one can take.
This silly carpenter began to quake;
Before his eyes there verily seemed to be
The floods of Noah, wallowing like the sea,
And drowning Alison, his honey-pet.
He wept and wailed, his features were all set
In grief, he sighed with many a doleful grunt;
He went and got a tub, began to hunt
For kneading-troughs, found two, and had them sent
Home to his house in secret; then he went
And, unbeknowns, he hung them from a rafter
With his own hands he made three ladders after,
Uprights and rungs, to help them in their scheme
Of climbing to the tubs upon the beam.
He victualled tub and trough, and made all snug
With bread and cheese, and ale in a large jug,
Enough for three of them, to last the day,
And just before completing this array,

He sente his knave, and eek his wenche also,
Up-on his nede to London for to go.
And on the Monday, whan it drow to night,
He shette his dore with-oute candel-light,
And dressed al thing as it sholde be.
And shortly, up they clomben alle three;
They sitten stille wel a furlong-way.

'Now, *Pater-noster, clom!*' seyde Nicholay,
And '*clom,*' quod John, and '*clom,*' seyde Alisoun.
This carpenter seyde his devocioun,
And stille he sit, and biddeth his preyere,
Awaytinge on the reyn, if he it here.

The dede sleep, for wery bisinesse,
Fil on this carpenter right, as I gesse,
Aboute corfew-tyme, or litel more;
For travail of his goost he groneth sore,
And eft he routeth, for his heed mislay.
Doun of the laddre stalketh Nicholay,
And Alisoun, ful softe adoun she spedde;
With-outen wordes mo, they goon to bedde
Ther-as the carpenter is wont to lye.
Ther was the revel and the melodye;
And thus lyth Alison and Nicholas,
In bisinesse of mirthe and of solas,
Til that the belle of laudes gan to ringe,
And freres in the chauncel gonne singe.

This parish-clerk, this amorous Absolon,
That is for love alwey so wo bigon,
Up-on the Monday was at Oseneye
With companye, him to disporte and pleye,
And axed up-on cas a cloisterer
Ful prively after John the carpenter;
And he drough him a-part out of the chirche,
And seyde, 'I noot, I saugh him here nat wirche
Sin Saterday; I trow that he be went
For timber, ther our abbot hath him sent;
For he is wont for timber for to go,
And dwellen at the grange a day or two;

Packed off the maid and the apprentice too
To London, on a job they had to do.
And on the Monday, when it drew to night,
He shut the door and dowsed the candle-light
And made quite sure all was as it should be.
And, shortly, up they clambered, all the three,
And waited there for what should come to pass.
Now *'Pater Noster . . . mum'* said Nicholas,
And *'mum'* said John and *'mum'* said Alison.
The carpenter's devotions being done,
He sat quite still, then fell to prayer again,
Listening anxiously to hear the rain,
But, weary with the work that he had seen,
Fell dead asleep—round curfew must have been,
Maybe a little later on the whole.
He groaned in sleep for travail of his soul,
And snored because his head was turned awry.

   Down by their ladders, stalking from on high,
Came Nicholas and Alison, and sped
Softly downstairs, without a word, to bed,
And where this carpenter was wont to be
The revels started and the melody.
And thus lay Nicholas and Alison
In solace, and were busy at their fun
Until the bell for lauds had started ringing,
And, in the chancel, friars began their singing.

   This parish clerk, this amorous Absalon,
Love-stricken still and ever woe-begone,
That very Monday was in company
At Osney with some fellows on the spree,
And chanced to ask a resident cloisterer
What had become of John the carpenter.
The fellow drew him out of church to say
'Don't know; not seen at work since Saturday;
Not sure, but I imagine that he went
To fetch the Abbot timber; he is sent
Often enough, and he is wont to go
Out to the Grange and stop a day or so;

Or elles he is at his hous, certeyn;
Wher that he be, I can nat sothly seyn.'

This Absolon ful joly was and light,
And thoghte, 'now is tyme wake al night;
For sikirly I saugh him nat stiringe
Aboute his dore sin day bigan to springe.
So moot I thryve, I shal, at cokkes crowe,
Ful prively knokken at his windowe
That stant ful lowe up-on his boures wal.
To Alison now wol I tellen al
My love-longing, for yet I shal nat misse
That at the leste wey I shal hir kisse.
Som maner confort shal I have, parfay,
My mouth hath icched al this longe day;
That is a signe of kissing atte leste.
Al night me mette eek, I was at a feste.
Therfor I wol gon slepe an houre or tweye,
And al the night than wol I wake and pleye.'

Whan that the firste cok hath crowe, anon
Up rist this joly lover Absolon,
And him arrayeth gay, at point-devys.
But first he cheweth greyn and lycorys,
To smellen swete, er he had kembd his heer.
Under his tonge a trewe love he beer,
For ther-by wende he to ben gracious.
He rometh to the carpenteres hous,
And stille he stant under the shot-windowe;
Un-to his brest it raughte, it was so lowe;
And softe he cogheth with a semi-soun—
'What do ye, hony-comb, swete Alisoun?
My faire brid, my swete cinamome,
Awaketh, lemman myn, and speketh to me!
Wel litel thenken ye up-on my wo,
That for your love I swete ther I go.
No wonder is thogh that I swelte and swete;
I moorne as doth a lamb after the tete.
Y-wis, lemman, I have swich love-longinge,
That lyk a turtel trewe is my moorninge;

[196]

If not, he's certainly at home to-day,
But where he is I can't exactly say.'
　Absalon was a jolly lad, and light
Of heart; he thought 'I'll stay awake to-night;
I'm certain that I haven't seen him stirring
About his door since dawn; it's safe inferring
That he's away. As I'm alive, I'll go
And tap his window softly at the crow
Of cock—the sill is low-set on the wall;
I shall see Alison and tell her all
My love-longing, and I can hardly miss
Some favour from her—at the least a kiss.
I'll get some satisfaction anyway;
There's been an itching in my mouth all day,
Which is a sign of kissing at the least,
And all last night I dreamt about a feast.
I think I'll go and sleep an hour or two
Then wake and have some fun; that's what I'll do.'
　The first cock crew at last, and thereupon
Up rose this jolly lover Absalon
In gayest garments—he was smart at this—
But first he chewed a grain of liquorice
To charm his breath, and then he combed his hair;
Under his tongue the comfit nestling there
Would make him gracious. He began to roam
To where old John and Alison kept home,
And by the casement window took his stand;
Breast-high it stood, no higher than his hand.
He gave a gentle cough, a semi-sound:
'Alison, honey-comb, are you around?
Sweet cinnamon, my little pretty bird,
Sweetheart, awake, and say a little word!
You seldom think of me in all my woe;
I sweat for love of you, where'er I go
No wonder if I sweat and pine and bleat,
Like any lambkin hungering for the teat;
Believe me, darling, I'm so deep in love
I croon with longing like a turtle-dove,

I may nat ete na more than a mayde.'

'Go fro the window, Jakke fool,' she sayde,
'As help me god, it wol nat be "com ba me,"
I love another, and elles I were to blame,
Wel bet than thee, by Jesu, Absolon!
Go forth thy wey, or I wol caste a ston,
And lat me slepe, a twenty devel wey!'

'Allas,' quod Absolon, 'and weylawey!
That trewe love was ever so yvel biset!
Than kisse me, sin it may be no bet,
For Jesus love and for the love of me.'

'Wiltow than go thy wey ther-with?' quod she.

'Ye, certes, lemman,' quod this Absolon.

'Thanne make thee redy,' quod she, 'I come anon;'
And un-to Nicholas she seyde stille,
'Now hust, and thou shalt laughen al thy fille.'

This Absolon doun sette him on his knees,
And seyde, 'I am a lord at alle degrees;
For after this I hope ther cometh more!
Lemman, thy grace, and swete brid, thyn ore!'

The window she undoth, and that in haste,
'Have do,' quod she, 'com of, and speed thee faste,
Lest that our neighebores thee espye.'

This Absolon gan wype his mouth ful drye;
Derk was the night as pich, or as the cole,
And at the window out she putte hir hole,
And Absolon, him fil no bet ne wers,
But with his mouth he kiste hir naked ers
Ful savoury, er he was war of this.

Abak he sterte, and thoghte it was amis,
For wel he wiste a womman hath no berd;
He felte a thing al rough and long y-herd,
And seyde, 'fy! allas! what have I do?'

'Tehee!' quod she, and clapte the window to;
And Absolon goth forth a sory pas.

'A berd, a berd!' quod hende Nicholas,
'By goddes *corpus*, this goth faire and weel!'

This sely Absolon herde every deel,

[198]

I eat as little as a girl at school.'
   She said 'You leave my window, you Tom-fool!
There's no come-up-and-kiss-me here for you;
I love another, and why shouldn't I too?
Better than you, by Jesu, Absalon!
Take yourself off, or I shall throw a stone,
And let me sleep; you can just go to Hell!'
   'Alas!' said Absalon, 'I knew it well;
True love is always mocked and girded at,
So kiss me if you can't do more than that,
For Jesu's love and for the love of me.'
'And if I do, will you be off?' said she;
'Promise you, darling!' answered Absalon.
'Get ready, then, I'm coming now, hang on!'
She answered him, and said under her breath
To Nicholas 'Hush, and you'll laugh to death!'
   This Absalon went down upon his knee,
'I am a lord in any case,' said he;
'I hope there's more to come, the plot may thicken;
Be gracious to me, love! Your mouth, my chicken!'
She flung the window open then in haste,
'Have done,' she said, 'come on, no time to waste,
The neighbours here are always on the spy.'
Absalon started wiping his mouth dry
Dark was the night as pitch, as black as coal,
And at the window out she put her hole,
And Absalon, so Fortune framed the farce,
Put up his mouth and kissed her naked arse
Most savourously, before he knew of this.
   And back he started; something was amiss,
That women have no beards he was aware,
Yet what he felt was rough and had long hair.
'What have I done?' he said 'can that be you?'
'Tee-hee' she cried, and clapped the window to;
Off went poor Absalon sadly through the dark;
'A beard! A beard!' said Nicholas the Spark,
'God's *corpus*, that was something like a joke!'
Absalon, overhearing what he spoke,

And on his lippe he gan for anger byte;
And to him-self he seyde, 'I shal thee quyte!'
  Who rubbeth now, who froteth now his lippes
With dust, with sond, with straw, with clooth, with chippes,
But Absolon, that seith ful ofte, 'allas!
My soule bitake I un-to Sathanas,
But me wer lever than al this toun,' quod he,
'Of this despyt awroken for to be!
Allas!' quod he, 'allas! I ne hadde y-bleynt!'
His hote love was cold and al y-queynt;
For fro that tyme that he had kiste hir ers,
Of paramours he sette nat a kers,
For he was heled of his maladye;
Ful ofte paramours he gan deffye,
And weep as dooth a child that is y-bete.
A softe paas he wente over the strete
Un-til a smith men cleped daun Gerveys,
That in his forge smithed plough-harneys;
He sharpeth shaar and culter bisily.
This Absolon knokketh al esily,
And seyde, 'undo, Gerveys, and that anon.'
  'What, who artow?' 'It am I, Absolon.'
'What, Absolon! for Cristes swete tree,
Why ryse ye so rathe, ey, *ben'cite!*
What eyleth yow? som gay gerl, god it woot,
Hath broght yow thus up-on the viritoot;
By sëynt Note, ye woot wel what I mene.'
  This Absolon ne roghte nat a bene
Of al his pley, no word agayn he yaf;
He hadde more tow on his distaf
Than Gerveys knew, and seyde, 'freend so dere,
That hote culter in the chimenee here,
As lene it me, I have ther-with to done,
And I wol bringe it thee agayn ful sone.'
  Gerveys answerde, 'certes, were it gold,
Or in a poke nobles alle untold,
Thou sholdest have, as I am trewe smith;

[200]

Said to himself in fury, as he bit
His lips with rage 'I'll pay you back for it!'
  Who's busy rubbing, scraping at his lips
With dust, with sand, with straw, with cloth, with chips,
But Absalon? He thought 'I'll bring him down!
I wouldn't let this go for all the town!
I'll take my soul and sell it to the Devil
To be revenged upon him! I'll get level.
Alas! why did I let myself be fooled?'
The fiery heat of love by now had cooled;
From the instant he had kissed her hinder parts
He had lost all his interest in tarts;
His malady was cured by this endeavour
And he defied all paramours whatever.
So, weeping like a child that has been whipped,
He turned away; across the street he slipped,
And called up Gervase; Gervase was a smith;
His forge was full of things for ploughing with,
And he was busy sharpening a share.
Absalon knocked, and with an easy air
Called 'Gervase! Open up the door, come on.'
'What? Who are you?' 'It's I, it's Absalon.'
'What, Absalon? By Jesu's blessed tree,
You're early up! Hey, *benedicite*,
What's wrong with you? Some girl, as like as not,
Has coaxed you out and set you on the trot;
Blessed St. Neot! You know the thing I mean.'
  But Absalon, who didn't give a bean
For all his joking, offered no debate;
He had a good deal more upon his plate
Than Gervase knew, and said 'Would it be fair
To borrow that coulter in the chimney there,
The hot one, friend? I've got a job to do;
It won't take long, I'll bring it back to you.'
  Gervase said 'Sure! If it were made of gold,
Or else a bag of sovereigns, wealth untold,
It should be yours, as I'm an honest smith;

Ey, Cristes foo! what wol ye do ther-with?'

'Ther-of,' quod Absolon, 'be as be may;
I shal wel telle it thee to-morwe day'—
And caughte the culter by the colde stele.
Ful softe out at the dore he gan to stele,
And wente un-to the carpenteres wal.
He cogheth first, and knokketh ther-with-al
Upon the windowe, right as he dide er.

This Alison answerde, 'Who is ther
That knokketh so? I warante it a theef.'

'Why, nay,' quod he, 'god woot, my swete leef,
I am thyn Absolon, my dereling!
Of gold,' quod he, 'I have thee broght a ring;
My moder yaf it me, so god me save,
Ful fyn it is, and ther-to wel y-grave;
This wol I yeve thee, if thou me kisse!'

This Nicholas was risen for to pisse,
And thoghte he wolde amenden al the jape,
He sholde kisse his ers er that he scape.
And up the windowe dide he hastily,
And out his ers he putteth prively
Over the buttok, to the haunche-bon;
And ther-with spak this clerk, this Absolon,
'Spek, swete brid, I noot nat wher thou art.'

This Nicholas anon leet flee a fart,
As greet as it had been a thonder-dent,
That with the strook he was almost y-blent;
And he was redy with his iren hoot,
And Nicholas amidde the ers he smoot.

Of gooth the skin an hande-brede aboute,
The hote culter brende so his toute,
And for the smert he wende for to dye.
As he were wood, for wo he gan to crye—
'Help! water! water! help, for goddes herte!'

This carpenter out of his slomber sterte,
And herde oon cryen 'water' as he were wood,
And thoghte, 'Allas! now comth Nowélis flood!'
He sit him up with-outen wordes mo,

[202]

But, Christ, why borrow *that* to do it with?'
'Let that' said Absalon 'be what it may;
You'll hear about it all some other day.'
He caught the coulter up—the haft was cool—
And left the smithy softly with the tool,
Crept to the little window in the wall,
And coughed; he knocked and gave a little call
Under the window as he had before.

    'Who's knocking so? Some thief is at the door!'
'Why, no,' he said 'my little flower-leaf,
I am your Absalon, beloved thing!
Look what I've brought you! It's a golden ring
My mother gave me, as I may be saved;
It's very fine and prettily engraved.
I'll give it to you, darling, for a kiss.'

    Now Nicholas had risen for a piss,
And thought he could improve upon the jape
And make him kiss his arse ere he escape,
And, opening the window with a jerk,
Stuck out his arse, a handsome piece of work,
Buttocks and all, as far as to the haunch.

    Said Absalon, all set to make a launch,
'Speak, pretty bird, I know not where thou art!'
This Nicholas at once let fly a fart
As loud as if it were a thunder-clap.
He was near blinded by the blast, poor chap,
But his hot iron was ready; with a thump
He smote him in the middle of the rump.
Off goes the skin, at least a hand's breadth wide,
The red-hot coulter scorching his backside;
The pain was terrible, he thought he'd die,
And, like a madman he began to cry
'Help! Water! Water! Help, for Heaven's love!'
This carpenter, starting from sleep above,
And hearing shouts for water and a thud,
Thought 'Heaven help us, here comes Nowel's Flood!'
And up he sat and with no more ado

And with his ax he smoot the corde a-two,
And doun goth al; he fond neither to selle,
Ne breed ne ale, til he cam to the selle
Up-on the floor; and ther aswowne he lay.

Up sterte hir Alison, and Nicholay,
And cryden 'out' and 'harrow' in the strete.
The neighebores, bothe smale and grete,
In ronnen, for to gauren on this man,
That yet aswowne he lay, bothe pale and wan;
For with the fal he brosten hadde his arm;
But stonde he moste un-to his owne harm.
For whan he spak, he was anon bore doun
With hende Nicholas and Alisoun.
They tolden every man that he was wood,
He was agast so of 'Nowélis flood'
Thurgh fantasye, that of his vanitee
He hadde y-boght him kneding-tubbes three,
And hadde hem hanged in the roof above;
And that he preyed hem, for goddes love,
To sitten in the roof, *par companye*.

The folk gan laughen at his fantasye;
In-to the roof they kyken and they gape,
And turned al his harm un-to a jape.
For what so that this carpenter answerde,
It was for noght, no man his reson herde;
With othes grete he was so sworn adoun,
That he was holden wood in al the toun;
For every clerk anon-right heeld with other.
They seyde, 'the man is wood, my leve brother;'
And every wight gan laughen of this stryf.

Thus swyved was the carpenteres wyf,
For al his keping and his jalousye;
And Absolon hath kist hir nether yë;
And Nicholas is scalded in the toute.
This tale is doon, and god save al the route!

[204]

He grabbed his axe and smote the ropes in two
And down went everything; he didn't stop
To sell his bread and ale, but came down flop
Upon the floor and fainted dead away.
  Up started Alison and Nicholay
And shouted 'Help!' and 'Murder!' in the street.
The neighbours, great and small, to see the treat
Came running in to stare at the poor man,
Where he lay swooning still, all pale and wan;
His arm in falling had been broken double,
But still he was obliged to face his trouble,
For when he spoke he was at once borne down
By Alison and Nicholas; the town
Was told that by some madness in his blood
He had a crazy fear of 'Nowel's Flood',
Mere fantasy, and in his vanity
He had bought kneading-tubs, and hanged them—three—
Among the rafters in the roof above
And he had begged them both for Heaven's love
To sit up in the roof for company.
  All started laughing at his fantasy
And streamed upstairs to gape and pry and poke,
And treated all his sufferings as a joke.
No matter what the carpenter asserted,
It went for nothing; no one was converted;
With powerful oaths they swore the fellow down
And he was held for mad by all the town;
And every scholar said to every other
'The fellow must be crazy, my dear brother!'
And they all laughed at this preposterous strife.
So much for carpenters! And thus his wife
Was plumbed, in spite of all his jealousy,
And Absalon has kissed her nether eye,
And Nicholas is branded on the bum.
And God bring all of us to Kingdom Come.

29. *The Canon's Yeoman's Tale*

lines 750–937, with omissions

Whan we been ther as we shul exercyse
Our elvish craft, we semen wonder wyse,
Our termes been so clergial and so queynte.
I blowe the fyr til that myn herte feynte.

What sholde I tellen ech proporcioun
Of thinges whiche that we werche upon,
As on fyve or sixe ounces, may wel be,
Of silver or som other quantitee,
And bisie me to telle yow the names
Of orpiment, brent bones, yren squames,
That into poudre grounden been ful smal?
And in an erthen potte how put is al,
And salt y-put in, and also papeer,
Biforn thise poudres that I speke of heer,
And wel y-covered with a lampe of glas,
And mochel other thing which that ther was?
And of the pot and glasses enluting,
That of the eyre mighte passe out no-thing?
And of the esy fyr and smart also,
Which that was maad, and of the care and wo
That we hadde in our matires sublyming,
And in amalgaming and calcening
Of quik-silver, y-clept Mercurie crude?
For alle our sleightes we can nat conclude.
Our orpiment and sublymed Mercurie,
Our grounden litarge eek on the porphurie,
Of ech of thise of ounces a certeyn
Nought helpeth us, our labour is in veyn.

THE WORLD OF SCIENCE

29. *How to be an Alchemist*

When we had fixed a place to exercise
Our esoteric craft, we all looked wise;
Our terms were highly technical and quaint.
I blew the fire up till fit to faint.
As for proportions, why should I go on
About the substances we worked upon,
The six or seven ounces, it may be,
Of silver, or some other quantity,
Or bother to name the things that we were piling
Up, such as arsenic, burnt bones, iron filing
Ground into finest powder, all the lot,
Or how we poured them in an earthen pot
(You put in salt and paper—is that clear?—
Before these powders that I speak of here
Securely covered by a sheet of glass,
And plenty of other things, but let them pass).
Then how the pot and glass were daubed with clay
For fear the gases might escape away,
And then the fire, whether slow or brisk,
We had to make, the trouble and the risk
We took to vaporise our preparation,
And in the amalgam and the calcination
Of quicksilver—crude mercury, that is.
We always failed, for all those tricks of his.
Our arsenic, our mercury sublimate,
Our lead protoxide, ground on a porphyry plate,
All measured out in ounces, grain by grain,
Gave us no help; our labour was in vain.

Ne eek our spirites ascencioun,
Ne our materes that lyen al fixe adoun,
Mowe in our werking no-thing us avayle.
For lost is al our labour and travayle,
And al the cost, a twenty devel weye,
Is lost also, which we upon it leye.

A! nay! lat be; the philosophres stoon,
Elixir clept, we sechen faste echoon;
I warne yow wel, it is to seken ever;
That futur temps hath maad men to dis-sever,
In trust ther-of, from al that ever they hadde.
Yet of that art they can nat wexen sadde,
And evermore, wher that ever they goon,
Men may hem knowe by smel of brim-stoon;
For al the world, they stinken as a goot;
Her savour is so rammish and so hoot,
That, though a man from hem a myle be,
The savour wol infecte him, trusteth me;

Passe over this; I go my tale un-to.
Er than the pot be on the fyr y-do,
Of metals with a certein quantitee,
My lord hem tempreth, and no man but he—
And wite ye how? ful ofte it happeth so,
The pot to-breketh, and farewel! al is go!
Thise metals been of so greet violence,
Our walles mowe nat make hem resistence,
But if they weren wroght of lym and stoon;
They percen so, and thurgh the wal they goon,
And somme of hem sinken in-to the ground—
Thus han we lost by tymes many a pound—
And somme are scatered al the floor aboute,
Somme lepe in-to the roof; with-outen doute,
Though that the feend noght in our sighte him shewe,
I trowe he with us be, that ilke shrewe!
In helle wher that he is lord and sire,
Nis ther more wo, ne more rancour ne ire.
Whan that our pot is broke, as I have sayd,
Every man chit, and halt him yvel apayd.

[208]

Neither the gas that rose as things grew hot,
Nor solids at the bottom of the pot,
Were the least use in what we tried to do;
Lost was our trouble, lost our labour too,
And all the money, in the name of Hell,
That we'd laid out on it was lost as well. . . .
Ah, no! To seek for the Philosophers' Stone,
Called the Elixir, that we long to own,
I give you warning, is to seek for ever,
A golden future lures one on to sever
Oneself from all one ever had, and trust
An art for which one cannot lose the lust. . . .

Go where they may, a man can always tell
These men of science by their brimstone smell;
For all the world they stink just like a goat,
A hot and ram-like smell that seems to float
About them, and a man a mile away
Will catch the foul infection, I dare say. . . .

Well, pass on to the story you require;
Before the pot is placed upon the fire
My Master takes a certain quantity
Of metals, which he tempers, none but he;
And how do you think? It happens, like as not,
There's an explosion, and good-bye the pot!
The metals are so violent when they split,
Our very walls can scarce stand up to it.
Unless well-built and made of stone and lime,
Bang go the metals through them every time,
And some are driven down into the ground
—That way we used to lose them by the pound!
And some are scattered all about the floor,
Some even jump into the roof, what's more.
Although the devil didn't show his face,
I'm pretty sure he was about the place.
In Hell itself, where he is lord and master,
There couldn't be more rancour in disaster
Than when our pots exploded, as I told you.
All think they've been let down and start to scold you.

Som seyde, it was long on the fyr-making,
Som seyde, nay! it was on the blowing;
(Than was I fered, for that was myn office);
'Straw!' quod the thridde, 'ye been lewed and nyce,
It was nat tempred as it oghte be.'
'Nay!' quod the ferthe, 'stint, and herkne me;
By-cause our fyr ne was nat maad of beech,
That is the cause, and other noon, so theech!'
I can nat telle wher-on it was long,
But wel I wot greet stryf is us among.

'What!' quod my lord, 'ther is na-more to done,
Of thise perils I wol be war eft-sone;
I am right siker that the pot was crased.
Be as be may, be ye no-thing amased;
As usage is, lat swepe the floor as swythe,
Plukke up your hertes, and beth gladde and blythe.'

Some say the way the fire was made was wrong;
And others, 'No! The bellows; blown too strong.'
(That frightened me, I blew them as a rule).
'Stuff!' says a third, 'You're nothing but a fool!
It wasn't tempered as it ought to be.'
'No,' says a fourth, 'Shut up and listen to me;
I say it should have been a beech-wood fire,
And that's the real cause, or I'm a liar.'

I'd no idea why the thing went wrong;
Recriminations, though, came hot and strong.
'Well,' says my Lord, 'there's nothing more to do;
I'll note these dangers for another brew;
I'm pretty certain that the pot was cracked;
Be that as may, don't gape! We've got to act.
Don't be alarmed, help to sweep up the floor,
Pluck up your hearts, cheer up, and try once more . . .!'

30. *The Merchant's Tale*

lines 93–110

A wyf! a! Seinte Marie, *ben'cite!*
How mighte a man han any adversitee
That hath a wyf? certes, I can nat seye.
The blisse which that is bitwixe hem tweye
Ther may no tonge telle, or herte thinke.
If he be povre, she helpeth him to swinke;
She kepeth his good, and wasteth never a deel;
Al that hir housbonde lust, hir lyketh weel;
She seith not ones 'nay,' when he seith 'ye.'
'Do this,' seith he; 'al redy, sir,' seith she.
O blisful ordre of wedlok precious,
Thou art so mery, and eek so vertuous,
And so commended and appreved eek,
That every man that halt him worth a leek,
Up-on his bare knees oghte al his lyf
Thanken his god that him hath sent a wyf;
Or elles preye to god him for to sende
A wyf, to laste un-to his lyves ende.

31. *The Merchant's Tale*

lines 67–74

A wyf is goddes yifte verraily;
Alle other maner yiftes hardily,

[212]

THE WORLD OF MATRIMONY

30. *What a Benediction!*

A wife! Saint Mary, what a benediction!
How can a man be subject to affliction
Who has a wife? Indeed I cannot say.
There is a bliss between them such as may
No tongue tell forth, such as no heart can judge.
If he be poor, she helps her man to drudge,
Sets guard on all his goods and checks the waste;
All that her husband likes is to her taste;
She never once says 'No' when he says 'Yes'.
'Do this' says he; 'already done!' she says.
O blissful state of wedlock, no way vicious,
But virtuous and merry, nay, delicious,
And so commended and approved by all
That any man who's worth a leek should fall
On his bare knees, to thank God, all his life,
For blessing him by sending him a wife,
Or else to pray that He vouchsafe to send
A wife to last him to the very end.

31. *The Gift of God*

A wife is verily the gift of God.
All other kinds of gift—the fruitful sod

As londes, rentes, pasture, or commune,
Or moebles, alle ben yiftes of fortune,
That passen as a shadwe upon a wal.
But dredelees, if pleynly speke I shal,
A wyf wol laste, and in thyn hous endure,
Wel lenger than thee list, paraventure.

32. *The Merchant's Tale*

lines 278–310

Senek among his othere wordes wyse
Seith, that a man oghte him right wel avyse,
To whom he yeveth his lond or his catel.
And sin I oghte avyse me right wel
To whom I yeve my good awey fro me,
Wel muchel more I oghte avysed be
To whom I yeve my body; for alwey
I warne yow wel, it is no childes pley
To take a wyf with-oute avysement.
Men moste enquere, this is myn assent,
Wher she be wys, or sobre, or dronkelewe,
Or proud, or elles other-weys a shrewe;
A chydester, or wastour of thy good,
Or riche, or poore, or elles mannish wood.
Al-be-it so that no man finden shal
Noon in this world that trotteth hool in al,
Ne man ne beest, swich as men coude devyse;
But nathelees, it oghte y-nough suffise
With any wyf, if so were that she hadde
Mo gode thewes than hir vyces badde;
And al this axeth leyser for t'enquere.
For god it woot, I have wept many a tere
Ful prively, sin I have had a wyf.

Of land, fair pastures, movables in store,
Rents—they're the gifts of Fortune, nothing more,
That pass as does a shadow on a wall.
Still, if I must speak plainly, after all,
A wife may last some time, and time may lapse
A good deal slower than one likes, perhaps.

32. *A More Cautious View*

Seneca gave a lot of sound advice;
He said it's always better to think twice
Before you give away estate or pelf.
And therefore, if you should advise yourself
In giving property away, or land,
If it's important you should understand
Who is to get your goods, how much the more
Ought you to think things over well, before
You give away your body. If I may,
I'd like to warn you; it is no child's play
Choosing a wife; it needs consideration;
In fact it asks a long investigation.
Is she discreet and sober? Or a drinker?
Or arrogant? Or shrewish like a tinker?
A scolder? Too extravagant? Too mannish?
Too poor? Too rich? Unnaturally clannish?
Although I know there isn't to be found
In all the world one that can trot quite sound,
Either in man or beast, the way we'd like it,
It were sufficient bargain, could we strike it
With any woman, were one sure she had
More good among her qualities than bad.

But all this asks some leisure to review;
God knows that many is the tear I too
Have wept in secret, since I had a wife.

Preyse who-so wole a wedded mannes lyf,
Certein, I finde in it but cost and care,
And observances, of alle blisses bare.
And yet, god woot, my neighebores aboute,
And namely of wommen many a route,
Seyn that I have the moste stedefast wyf,
And eek the mekeste oon that bereth lyf.
But I wot best wher wringeth me my sho.
Ye mowe, for me, right as yow lyketh do;

33. *The Merchant's Tale*

lines 393–408

I have,' quod he, 'herd seyd, ful yore ago,
Ther may no man han parfite blisses two,
This is to seye, in erthe and eek in hevene.
For though he kepe him fro the sinnes sevene,
And eek from every branche of thilke tree,
Yet is ther so parfit felicitee,
And so greet ese and lust in mariage,
That ever I am agast, now in myn age,
That I shal lede now so mery a lyf,
So delicat, with-outen wo and stryf,
That I shal have myn hevene in erthe here.
For sith that verray hevene is boght so dere,
With tribulacioun and greet penaunce,
How sholde I thanne, that live in swich plesaunce
As alle wedded men don with hir wyvis,
Come to the blisse ther Crist eterne on lyve is?

[216]

Praise whoso will the married state of life,
I find it a routine, a synthesis
Of cost and care, and wholly bare of bliss.
And yet the neighbours, all of them, by God,
Especially the women—in a squad—
Congratulate me that I chose to wive
The constantest, the meekest soul alive.
I know where the shoe pinches; but for you,
Why, you must please yourself in what you do.

33. Two Perfect Kinds of Bliss

But I have often heard it said ere this
That none may have two perfect kinds of bliss,
Bliss in this world, I mean, and bliss in Heaven;
Though he keep clear of sin—the Deadly Seven,
And all the branches of their dreadful tree—
Yet there's so perfect a felicity
In marriage, so much pleasure, so few tears,
Even for those that are advanced in years
I shall be leading such a happy life,
So delicate, with neither grief nor strife,
That I shall have my Heaven here in earth;
And may not that cost more than it is worth?
Since that true Heaven costs a man so dear
In tribulation and in penance here,
How should one then, living in such delight
As every married man by day and night
Lives with his wife, attain to joys supernal,
And enter into bliss with Christ Eternal?

34. *The Merchant's Tale*

lines 411–438

Justinus, which that hated his folye,
Answerde anon, right in his japerye;
And for he wolde his longe tale abregge,
He wolde noon auctoritee allegge,
But seyde, 'sire, so ther be noon obstacle
Other than this, god of his hye miracle
And of his mercy may so for yow wirche,
That, er ye have your right of holy chirche,
Ye may repente of wedded mannes lyf,
In which ye seyn ther is no wo ne stryf.
And elles, god forbede but he sente
A wedded man him grace to repente
Wel ofte rather than a sengle man!
And therfore, sire, the beste reed I can,
Dispeire yow noght, but have in your memorie,
Paraunter she may be your purgatorie!
She may be goddes mene, and goddes whippe;
Than shal your soule up to hevene skippe
Swifter than dooth an arwe out of the bowe!
I hope to god, her-after shul ye knowe,
That their nis no so greet felicitee
In mariage, ne never-mo shal be,
That yow shal lette of your savacioun,
So that ye use, as skile is and resoun,
The lustes of your wyf attemprely,
And that ye plese hir nat to amorously,
And that ye kepe yow eek from other sinne.
My tale is doon:—for my wit is thinne.

34. *God's Whip*

Justinus, who despised this nonsense, said,
Jesting as ever, what was in his head;
And wishing not to spin things out in chatter,
Used no authorities to support his matter.
'If there's no obstacle,' he said 'but this,
God, by some mighty miracle of His,
May show His mercy, as He is wont to do,
And, long before they come to bury you,
You may repent you of your married life
In which you say there never can be strife;
And God forbid that there should not be sent
A special grace for husbands, to repent,
And sent more often than to single men!
This, Sir, would be my own conclusion, then;
Never despair! You still may go to glory;
Your wife, perhaps, may prove your purgatory,
God's means of grace, as one might say, God's whip,
To send your soul to Heaven with a skip,
And swifter than an arrow from the bow!
I hope to God that you may shortly know
That there is no such great felicity
In marriage, nor is ever like to be,
As to disqualify you for salvation,
Provided you observe some moderation,
Tempering down the passions of your wife,
With some restriction on your amorous life,
Keeping yourself, of course, from other sin.
My tale is done, but there! My wit is thin.

35. *From the Wife of Bath's Prologue*

lines 1–614, with omissions

'Experience, though noon auctoritee
Were in this world, were right y-nough to me
To speke of wo that is in mariage;
For, lordinges, sith I twelf yeer was of age,
Thonked be god that is eterne on lyve,
Housbondes at chirche-dore I have had fyve;
But me was told certeyn, nat longe agon is,
That sith that Crist ne wente never but onis
To wedding in the Cane of Galilee,
That by the same ensample taughte he me
That I ne sholde wedded be but ones.
Herke eek, lo! which a sharp word for the nones
Besyde a welle Jesus, god and man,
Spak in repreve of the Samaritan:
"Thou hast y-had fyve housbondes," quod he,
"And thilke man, the which that hath now thee,
Is noght thyn housbond;" thus seyde he certeyn;
What that he mente ther-by, I can nat seyn;
But that I axe, why that the fifthe man
Was noon housbond to the Samaritan?
How manye mighte she have in mariage?
Yet herde I never tellen in myn age
Upon this nombre diffinicioun;
Men may devyne and glosen up and doun.
But wel I woot expres, with-oute lye,
God bad us for to wexe and multiplye;
That gentil text can I wel understonde.
Eek wel I woot he seyde, myn housbonde
Sholde lete fader and moder, and take me;

35. *From the Memoirs of the Wife of Bath*

If there were no authority on earth
Except experience, mine, for what it's worth,
Would be enough, enough at least for me,
To speak of marriage and its misery.
For let me say, if I may make so bold,
My lords, since when I was but twelve years old,
(Thanks be to God Eternal evermore!)
Five husbands have I had at the church door.
Someone said recently, for my persuasion,
That as Christ only went on one occasion
To grace a wedding—in Cana of Gallilee—
By this example he was teaching me
That it is wrong to marry more than once.
Consider, too, how sharply, for the nonce,
He spoke, rebuking the Samaritan
Beside the well—Christ Jesus, God and man.
'Thou hast had five men husband unto thee,
And he that even now thou hast' said He
'Is not thy husband'. Thus the saying fell;
But what He meant by it I cannot tell.
Why was her fifth—explain it if you can—
No husband to her—the Samaritan?
How many might have had her, then, to wife?
I've never heard the answer all my life
That gives the number final definition;
One may expound or frame a supposition,
But I can say for certain, and no lie,
God bade us all to wax and multiply;
That noble text I well can understand.
Is not my husband under God's command
To leave his father and mother, and take me?

[221]

But of no nombre mencioun made he,
Of bigamye or of octogamye;
Why sholde men speke of it vileinye?

* * *

For hadde god comanded maydenhede,
Thanne hadde he dampned wedding with the dede;
And certes, if ther were no seed y-sowe,
Virginitee, wher-of than sholde it growe?

* * *

Crist was a mayde, and shapen as a man,
And many a seint, sith that the world bigan,
Yet lived they ever in parfit chastitee.
I nil envye no virginitee;
Lat hem be breed of pured whete-seed,
And lat us wyves hoten barly-breed;
And yet with barly-breed, Mark telle can,
Our lord Jesu refresshed many a man.

* * *

In wyfhode I wol use myn instrument
As frely as my maker hath it sent.
If I be daungerous, god yeve me sorwe!
Myn housbond shal it have bothe eve and morwe,
Whan that him list com forth and paye his dette.
An housbonde I wol have, I nil nat lette,
Which shal be bothe my dettour and my thral,
And have his tribulacioun with-al
Up-on his flessh, whyl that I am his wyf.
I have the power duringe al my lyf
Up-on his propre body, and noght he.
Right thus th'apostel tolde it un-to me;
And bad our housbondes for to love us weel.

* * *

I shal seye sooth, tho housbondes that I hadde,
As three of hem were gode and two were badde.

[222]

No word of what the number was to be,
Whether to marry two or marry eight;
So why speak evil of the married state?

*   *   *

Had God commanded maidenhood to all,
Then marriage had been damned beyond recall;
And certainly, if seed were never sown,
How ever could virginity be grown?

*   *   *

Christ was a virgin, fashioned as a man,
And saints a many since the world began
Lived ever perfectly in chastity;
I have no quarrel with virginity.
Let them be pure wheat loaves of maidenhead,
And let us wives be known as barley-bread;
Yet Mark can tell that barley-bread sufficed
To freshen many at the hand of Christ.

*   *   *

In wifehood I will use my instrument
As freely as my Maker me it sent;
If I turn difficult, God give me sorrow!
My husband—he shall have it, eve and morrow,
Whenever he likes to come and pay his debt.
I won't prevent him, I'll have a husband yet
Who shall be both my debtor and my slave
And bear his tribulation to the grave
Upon his flesh, as long as I'm his wife,
For mine shall be the power, all my life,
Over his proper body, and not he,
As the Apostle Paul has told it me,
And bade our husbands they should love us well . . .

*   *   *

I'll tell the truth. Those husbands that I had,
Three of them were good, and two were bad.

The three men were gode, and riche, and olde;
Unnethe mighte they the statut holde
In which that they were bounden un-to me.
Ye woot wel what I mene of this, pardee!
As help me god, I laughe whan I thinke
How pitously a-night I made hem swinke;
And by my fey, I tolde of it no stoor.
They had me yeven hir gold and hir tresoor;
Me neded nat do lenger diligence
To winne hir love, or doon hem reverence.
They loved me so wel, by god above,
That I ne tolde no deyntee of hir love!

* * *

For god it woot, I chidde hem spitously.
  Now herkneth, how I bar me proprely,
Ye wyse wyves, that can understonde.
  Thus shul ye speke and bere hem wrong on honde;
A wys wyf, if that she can hir good,
Shal beren him on hond the cow is wood,
    but herkneth how I sayde.
"Sir olde kaynard, is this thyn array?
Why is my neighebores wyf so gay?
She is honoured over-al ther she goth;
I sitte at hoom, I have no thrifty cloth.
What dostow at my neighebores hous?
Is she so fair? artow so amorous?
What rowne ye with our mayde? *ben' cite!*
Sir olde lechour, lat thy japes be!
And if I have a gossib or a freend,
With-outen gilt, thou chydest as a feend,
If that I walke or pleye un-to his hous!
Thou comest hoom as dronken as a mous,
And prechest on thy bench, with yvel preef!
Thou seist to me, it is a greet meschief
To wedde a povre womman, for costage;
And if that she be riche, of heigh parage,
Than seistow that it is a tormentrye

The three that I call good were rich and old;
They could indeed with difficulty hold
The articles that bound them all to me
(No doubt you understand my simile).
So help me God, I have to laugh outright,
How piteously I made them toil by night!
And faith, I set no store by it; no pleasure
It was to me; they'd given me their treasure;
I had no need to show more diligence
To win their love, or do them reverence.
They loved me well enough, so, Heavens above!
Why should I make a dainty of their love?

* * *

God knows how spitefully I used to scold them!
Listen, I'll tell you how I used to hold them,
You knowing women, that can understand.
First, put them in the wrong, and out of hand . . .
Now listen; here's the sort of thing I said:
"So that's your attitude, Sir Dotard, eh?
Why is my neighbour's wife so smart and gay?
She is respected everywhere she goes;
I sit at home and have no decent clothes.
Why do you haunt her house? What's doing there?
Are you so amorous, is she so fair?
What, are you whispering to our maid? For shame,
Sir Ancient lecher! Time you dropped that game.
And if I have a friend—all on the level—
Or gossip, why you scold me like the devil
If I so much as stroll towards his house;
You come home drunk, as drunk as any mouse,
You mount your throne and preach, with chapter and
    verse,
—(All nonsense)—and you tell me it's a curse
To marry a poor woman, for she's expensive;
But, if her family's wealthy and extensive,
You say it's torture to endure her pride
And melancholy airs, and more beside;

To suffre hir pryde and hir malencolye.
And if that she be fair, thou verray knave,
Thou seyst that every holour wol hir have;
She may no whyle in chastitee abyde,
That is assailled up-on ech a syde.

    Thou seyst, som folk desyre us for richesse,
Som for our shap, and som for our fairnesse;
And som, for she can outher singe or daunce,
And som, for gentillesse and daliaunce;
Som, for hir handes and hir armes smale;
Thus goth al to the devel by thy tale.

    Thou seist, that oxen, asses, hors, and houndes,
They been assayed at diverse stoundes;
Bacins, lavours, er that men hem bye,
Spones and stoles, and al swich housbondrye,
And so been pottes, clothes, and array;
But folk of wyves maken noon assay
Til they be wedded; olde dotard shrewe!
And than, seistow, we wol oure vices shewe.

*   *   *

    But, lord Crist! whan that it remembreth me
Up-on my yowthe, and on my jolitee,
It tikleth me aboute myn herte rote.
Unto this day it dooth myn herte bote
That I have had my world as in my tyme.
But age, allas! that al wol envenyme,
Hath me biraft my beautee and my pith;
Lat go, fare-wel, the devel go therwith!

*   *   *

For certes, I am al Venerien
In felinge, and myn herte is Marcien.
Venus me yaf my lust, my likerousnesse,
And Mars yaf me my sturdy hardinesse.
Myn ascendent was Taur, and Mars therinne.
Allas! allas! that ever love was sinne!

And if she has a pretty face, old traitor,
You say she's game for any fornicator,
And ask if she is likely to keep straight
With all those men who lie about in wait.
You say that some desire us for our money,
Some for our shape, some for a taste of honey,
Some for our singing, others for our dancing,
Some for our gentleness and dalliant glancing,
And some because their hands are soft and small;
By your account the devil gets us all. . . .
   You say that oxen, asses, hounds and horses
Can be tried out on various ploys and courses;
And basins too, and dishes, when you buy them,
Spoons, stools and furnishings—a man can try them,
And pots and pans and suits of clothes, no doubt,
But no one ever tries a woman out
Until he's married her; old dotard crow!
And then, you say, she lets her vices show.

*   *   *

Lord Christ! Whenever it comes back to me,
When I recall my youth and jollity,
It fairly warms the cockles of my heart!
And to this day I feel the pleasure start,
Yes, I can feel it tickle at the root;
It does me good that I have had my fruit,
I've had my world and time, I've had my fling!
But age, that comes to poison everything,
Has taken all my beauty and my pith;
Well, let it go, the devil go therewith!

*   *   *

Venus sent me feeling from the stars,
And my heart's boldness came to me from Mars;
Venus gave me desire and lecherousness,
And Mars my hardihood, or so I guess,
Born under Taurus and with Mars therein.
Alas, alas, that ever love was sin!

36. The Clerk of Oxford's Tale: Lenvoy de Chaucer

lines 1177–1212

Grisilde is deed, and eek hir pacience,
And bothe atones buried in Itaille;
For which I crye in open audience,
No wedded man so hardy be t'assaille
His wyves pacience, in hope to finde
Grisildes, for in certein he shall faille!

O noble wyves, ful of heigh prudence,
Lat noon humilitee your tonge naille,
Ne lat no clerk have cause or diligence
To wryte of yow a storie of swich mervaille
As of Grisildis pacient and kinde;
Lest Chichevache yow swelwe in hir entraille!

Folweth Ekko, that holdeth no silence,
But evere answereth at the countretaille;
Beth nat bidaffed for your innocence,
But sharply tak on yow the governaille.
Emprinteth wel this lesson in your minde
For commune profit, sith it may availle.

Ye archewyves, stondeth at defence,
Sin ye be stronge as is a greet camaille;
Ne suffreth nat that men yow doon offence.
And sclendre wyves, feble as in bataille,
Beth egre as is a tygre yond in Inde;
Ay clappeth as a mille, I yow consaille.

36. Anthem for Militant Wives

Griselda and her patience both are dead
And buried in some far Italian vale;
Be it proclaimed in court to all that wed:
'Husbands, be not so hardy as to assail
The patience of your wives in hope to find
Griseldas, for you certainly will fail!

O noble wives, in highest prudence bred,
Allow no such humility to nail
Your tongues, or give a scholar cause to shed
Such light on you as this astounding tale
Sheds on Griselda, patient still, and kind,
Lest Chichevache* engulf you like a whale.

Imitate Echo, she that never fled
In silence, but returns you hail for hail;
Never let innocence besot your head,
But take the helm yourself and trim the sail,
And print this lesson firmly in your head
For common profit; it can never stale.

Arch-wives, stand up! Defend your board and bed!
Stronger than camels as you are, prevail!
Don't swallow insults, offer them instead!
And all you slender little wives and frail,
Be fierce as Indian tigers, since designed
To rattle like a windmill in a gale.

---

* *Chichevache was a fabulous cow that lived on patient wives; so she was very thin. Bicorne, however, another such monster, ate patient husbands, and was stout.*

Ne dreed hem nat, do hem no reverence;
For though thyn housbonde armed be in maille,
The arwes of thy crabbed eloquence
Shal perce his brest, and eek his aventaille;
In jalousye I rede eek thou him binde,
And thou shalt make him couche as dooth a quaille.

If thou be fair, ther folk ben in presence
Shew thou thy visage and thyn apparaille;
If thou be foul, be free of thy dispence,
To gete thee freendes ay do thy travaille;
Be ay of chere as light as leef on linde,
And lat him care, and wepe, and wringe, and waille!

37. *The Franklin's Tale*

lines 33–50

For o thing, sires, saufly dar I seye,
That frendes everich other moot obeye,
If they wol longe holden companye.
Love wol nat ben constreyned by maistrye;
Whan maistrie comth the god of love anon
Beteth his winges, and farewel! he is gon!
Love is a thing as any spirit free;
Wommen of kinde desiren libertee,
And nat to ben constreyned as a thral;
And so don men, if I soth seyen shal.
Loke who that is most pacient in love,
He is at his avantage al above.
Pacience is an heigh vertu certeyn;
For it venquisseth, as thise clerkes seyn,
Thinges that rigour sholde never atteyne.
For every word men may nat chyde or pleyne.
Lerneth to suffre, or elles, so moot I goon,
Ye shul it lerne, wher-so ye wole or noon.

Never revere them, never stand in dread,
For though your husband wears a coat of mail,
Your shafts of crabbed eloquence will thread
His armour through and drub him like a flail.
And be suspicious of him! Guilt will bind
Him down, he'll couch as quiet as a quail.

If you are beautiful, advance your tread,
Show yourself off to people, blaze the trail!
If you are ugly, spend and make a spread,
Get friends to do the business of a male,
Dance like a linden-leaf if so inclined;
Leave him to weep and wring his hands and wail!

37. *When Love Beats his Wings*

For there's one thing, my lords, it's safe to say;
Lovers must each be ready to obey
The other, if they would long keep company.
Love will not be constrained by mastery;
When mastery comes, the god of love anon
Will beat his wings, and farewell! he is gone!
Love is a thing as any spirit free;
Women by nature long for liberty,
And not to be constrained, or made a thrall;
And so do men, if I may speak for all.
Whoever is most patient under love
Has the advantage and will rise above
The other; surely patience is a virtue.
The learned say that, if it not desert you,
It vanquishes where force could never reach;
Why answer back at every angry speech?
Learn to forbear, or else, I'll tell you what,
You will be taught it, whether you like or not.

38. Balade de bon conseyl

Flee fro the prees, and dwelle with sothfastnesse,
Suffyce unto thy good, though hit be smal;
For hord hath hate, and climbing tikelnesse,
Prees hath envye, and wele blent overal;
Savour no more than thee bihove shal;
Werk wel thy-self, that other folk canst rede;
And trouthe shal delivere, hit is no drede.

Tempest thee noght al croked to redresse,
In trust of hir that turneth as a bal:
Gret reste stant in litel besinesse;
And eek be war to sporne ageyn an al;
Stryve noght, as doth the crokke with the wal.
Daunte thy-self, that dauntest otheres dede;
And trouthe shal delivere, hit is no drede.

That thee is sent, receyve in buxumnesse,
The wrastling for this worlde axeth a fal.
Her nis non hoom, her nis but wildernesse:
Forth, pilgrim, forth! Forth, beste, out of thy stal!
Know thy contree, look up, thank God of al;
Hold the hye wey, and lat thy gost thee lede:
And trouthe shal delivere, hit is no drede.

EPILOGUE

38. *Forth, Pilgrim!*

Dwell in the truth, and to the throng be stranger,
Letting your means suffice, though they be small;
To hoard breeds hate, and climbing up is danger,
The throng is envious; riches blind us all.
Do not desire more than there is call,
Work well; in guiding others, self-severe.
Truth will be your deliverer, never fear.

And do not be tempestuous to redress
All that is crooked, trust not Fortune's tricks;
There is great peace in unofficiousness;
Be careful, les you kick against the pricks,
Or strive, like crockery, with a wall of bricks.
Subdue yourself, subduing others here;
Truth will be your deliverer, never fear.

Take what is sent in willing thankfulness;
To wrestle with the world invites a fall.
Here is no home, here's but a wilderness;
Forth, pilgrim, forth! Forth, beast, out of your stall!
Look upward, know your home, thank God for all;
Hold the high way and let your soul lead clear;
Truth shall be your deliverer, never fear.

Envoy

Therfore, thou vache, leve thyn old wrecchednesse
Unto the worlde; leve now to be thral;
Crye him mercy, that of his hy goodnesse
Made thee of noght, and in especial
Draw unto him, and pray in general
For thee, and eek for other, hevenlich mede;
And trouthe shal delivere, hit is no drede.

Envoi

And so, friend Vache,* leave your old wretchedness
Of thraldom to the world; enough, let be!
Cry mercy of Him that in his high goodness,
Made you from nothing; and especially
Draw near to Him in prayer, for you and me
And others too, for Heaven's reward and cheer;
Truth will be your deliverer, never fear!

(For Martin Starkie)

---

* *Sir Philip de la Vache (1346–1408) was a close friend of Chaucer's. He was keeper of the King's Manor and park of Chiltern Langley, but, like Chaucer, fell from favour between 1386–90, during the absence of John of Gaunt in Spain, when the Duke of Gloucester dominated the government of the young King Richard II. It may be that this poem reflects this situation.*